Dear Teenager, You Are Amazing

5 Keys to Creating a Life You Love

By

Blythe Metz-Mändmets, Ph.D.

©2023

Published by BNL Press
Los Angeles, Ca.
USA

Cover Design by Rajiv Verma, rkv4ever@gmail.com

Editing by Steph White (Kat's Literary Services)

Proofreading by Vanessa Esquibel (Kat's Literary Services)

Book formatted by Sara Sardar at CM Graphics Hub

ISBN: 979-8-89217-241-7

For permission or speaking requests, contact the author at Blythe@BlytheNaturalLiving.com.

First Edition: 12/23
Printed in USA

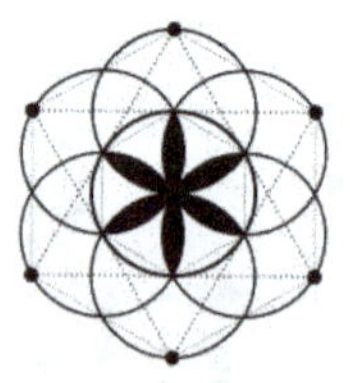

Dedicated to
Kate Malmen Ford

(1977-1996)

Your magic lives on in your son and in our memory.

If only you knew.

Table of Contents

Acknowledgments

I extend my deepest gratitude to you, the reader, for embarking on this journey with me. Without your engagement, the time, energy, focus and heart that went into writing this book would be wasted. I trust within these pages, you will discover the power within you to shape the life you desire. As you put into practice the insights shared here, your inherent genius will guide you.

To my beloved husband, daughter, and son, I owe immeasurable thanks. Their understanding and support during the creation of this book allowed for the solitary moments I needed to bring these ideas to life. Many family fun days were spent without my presence, and yet, their unwavering encouragement fueled my endeavors. My 8-year-old's reminder of our first family beach day in October this year serves as a poignant testament to their patience and understanding. I am profoundly grateful for their grace as I invested my time in this endeavor.

Special appreciation goes to my exceptional editors at Kat's Literary, Steph White, and Vanessa Esquibel, and to Sara Sardar from CM Graphics Hub for her exceptional work formatting this book.

Their keen insights, meticulous attention to detail, and unwavering commitment to excellence have enriched this book.

Once again, thank you, dear reader, and to all those who played a part in bringing this vision to life. May the wisdom within these pages inspire and empower you on your personal journey of growth and transformation.

Chapter 1
1st Key
Cultivating Unconditional Self-Love

Dear Teenager, You are amazing. Like really amazing. You don't have to impress me one bit. I'm already a big fan of yours. I know you. I know what you are capable of by being human. Simply BE-ing human. You have power you are likely unaware of but will fully embrace by the time you finish reading this book.

Before diving into the quantum field that your heart, brain, and gut are intimately connected to, that is most available to you in a position of unconditional self-love, I want to share with you some facts about the physical and metaphysical body that you occupy. I want you to fall deeply in love and awe for the amazing being you are. You are truly AWEsome.

Have you ever thought about how your eyeballs work? It's astounding. So complex and precise. Your eyeballs are one of the most amazing technologies on the planet, even if you wear eyeglasses. Have you pondered just how many cells are at work in your body? About 38 trillion cells, each with their own consciousness, electromagnetically communicating with each other, doing their job without your conscious effort or awareness. Did you know that about 98 percent of your body is made of microorganisms? Wow, right? So, YOU are a universe for this massive community of intelligent microorganisms that function as a human body and mind.

We are also metaphysical beings. Our thoughts and feelings create and change our bodies and environments. So the physical body functions automatically but can be commanded and transformed through conscious and unconscious mental and emotional patterns. This is how much power you have over your health, success, and life. Most people don't know this, or they learn it after they are already suffering in life. Learning this information as a teenager will allow you to chart a long, strong, vital life. I'm excited for you.

I love what Marianne Williamson says in her bestselling book *A Return to Love.* She writes, "Love taken seriously is a radical outlook, a major departure from the psychological orientation that rules the world." She goes on to explain that God is the energy, the thought of unconditional love. She continues, "*A Course in Miracles* calls itself a 'mind-training' in the relinquishment of a thought system based on fear, and the acceptance instead of a thought system based on love... Without love, we have no wisdom."

A Return to Love is on my must-read list for sure. I gave my first copy of this book to an incredible sixteen-year-old boy I met on El Matador beach in Malibu back in 2008. He had built himself a truly beautiful hut. This was back before social media and travel blogs gave our sweet, quiet beach worldwide recognition, making it a must-see destination in Southern California. But back then, it was quiet and undisturbed, and he was able to find sticks and stones and literally make himself a delightful two-room hut with a mailbox, to provide some relief from life. You see, only a couple of weeks before we met, he had made the choice to drive his car off an overpass to end his life. It did not work; he left the accident and his totaled car with barely a scratch on him. I was too young then to know the right thing to say to a teenage boy who was struggling so much to understand why bad things happen in the world. He was wearing the weight of the world and couldn't bear it. I went home and got my copy of *A Return to Love*, all highlighted and noted in the margins. When I returned to the beach, his parents were there with him, and I felt that it was a family moment, so I just gave him the book and left him. I pray he is doing amazing things in the world today. It's clear Life still needed him.

I know that the wisdom and guidance I have received from books have enhanced my life in every way. I'm writing this book for no other reason than to empower and enhance your life. We are not put here to struggle; we are put here to love, to create, to learn what we are made of, to enjoy that, and to share it with others.

> We are not put here to struggle; we are put here to love, to create, to learn what we are made of, to enjoy that, and to share it with others.

I read a book called *Love: What Life Is All About* by Leo Buscaglia when I was in high school. As I look back, I'm quite grateful that this was required reading for tenth graders. I remember sitting in my classroom and reading the words, "Others can only love you to the degree to which you love yourself." I always remember that, and I think it served me very well. Looking back at two and a half decades post-high school, I can see that I only had really kind and wonderful guys in my life. I had the best boyfriends. Every boyfriend I left, I left loving him. Or shall I say, every relationship that ended, it ended with love and respect intact but with the awareness that change was upon us. I was always ready for growth. I think that the more rooted you are in unconditional self-love, the easier it is to go into the unknown.

So, let's dive into unconditional self-love. I hear you inwardly asking, what is unconditional self-love exactly? Unconditional self-love is the basis for all health and wealth and everything good in between, especially good relationships.

First, I know that in the teenage years, we tend to get a lot of our validation from our peers and, these days, from social media. After tuning into unconditional self-love, you will not need any outside validation. You will fully embody your amazingness from within, completely impervious to other's opinions. That is a rock star feeling, and that happens naturally when practicing the principles of unconditional self-love that we will discuss in this chapter.

For many of us, it's hard to know what unconditional self-love feels like because we haven't *felt* unconditional love from others. I remember what it felt like the first time I received unconditional love from another person. I'll be honest, I didn't grow up feeling unconditional love from my parents or grandparents. Perhaps they felt unconditional love for me, but I did not feel that. I felt all the conditions. I felt the yelling, irritation, and annoyance that seemed to plague my parents. I felt the blows.

The first time I felt real unconditional love was from a friend in my early twenties. I could be completely, unapologetically real with her, and she loved me no matter what. I called her out on her inconsistencies and blind spots and witnessed her brilliance with a tough-love style of friendship. She never expressed any energy toward me that wasn't totally loving and accepting of me, even when I wasn't loving and accepting of myself.

Growing up in Illinois in the eighties, there wasn't any talk of self-love, only the firm stance to not be full of oneself or conceited. Such instruction felt like the opposite of self-love; "Don't shine too bright, don't stand out, you don't want to make others feel uncomfortable." I didn't receive any talks from my parents or teachers about loving myself and taking care of my mental, emotional, and physical body. This was something I figured out on my own as an adult, as many people do. I'm hoping to save you much time and energy and change the trajectory of your life by teaching you some profound principles in your teenage years that will help you create the life you want. Reading this book will equip you with the wisdom you need to take control of your mind, emotions, and life, and it's really fun.

I define unconditional self-love as a feeling of worthiness, acceptance, and value, regardless of what is happening in one's environment at the time. Regardless of performance, relationships, or merit, one feels love and acceptance for oneself by choice. This comes from within. You just decide I'm going to honor my mind, body, and spirit, and if I don't in a moment, I love myself anyway. I'm going to nourish my mind, body, and spirit, and if I don't in a moment, I'm going to love myself anyway. When I make mistakes, as we all do, I'm going to forgive myself immediately and look for the lesson. Unconditional self-love says, "I know I'll make mistakes, and I'll learn from them and be better for them." Unconditional self-love says, "I love myself even though I'm still figuring out who I am. I'm going to love myself on the way to becoming myself." It takes a lifetime to become yourself; don't expect to totally know your views on everything at your age or have complete command of your talents and interests. These things will develop over decades. Love yourself enough to trust your talents and continue to cultivate them. Love yourself enough to trust that what you truly enjoy doing in life is part of your destiny. Those are the two ways your destiny is revealed to you. Follow your talents and your joy, and you will align with your purpose on the planet and live richly.

> Follow your talents and your joy, and you will align with your purpose on the planet and live richly.

That's right, your PURPOSE (and there are many). Love yourself enough to know that you are crucial to the fullness of Life expression on the planet. You create energy by thinking and feeling; this energy contributes to the field that everything is connected to. So your thoughts and feelings are vibrating out a signal and affecting your environment. This is how powerful and important you are, not only in your own immediate environment but in the whole collective field.

> You create energy by thinking and feeling; this energy contributes to the field that everything is connected to. So your thoughts and feelings are vibrating out a signal and affecting your environment. This is how powerful and important you are, not only in your own immediate environment but in the whole collective field.

Practicing unconditional self-love does two main things: it helps you create and hardwire self-love in your brain so you consciously and unconsciously deeply love and accept yourself, and it ensures your body is operating in the parasympathetic nervous system. The parasympathetic nervous system is where you need to be to regenerate optimally, AKA stay youthful and healthy. Ever notice that people who stress a lot age a lot faster? That's because, on a biochemical level, they are producing stress hormones that keep the body in fight, flight, or freeze instead of rest and digest. Rest and digest is where the body repairs. Do you know someone who gets angry and has stomach issues? Anger or any form of stress produces chemicals in the body that pause digestion so that all the body's energy is focused on the stress. This is a very unhealthy place to live and will create disease in time because that's what dis-ease is.

The chemicals produced in your body when you unconditionally love yourself are the chemicals that keep you looking and feeling beautiful, inside and out.

> The chemicals produced in your body when you unconditionally love yourself are the chemicals that keep you looking and feeling beautiful, inside and out.

Did you know that your body regenerates in its entirety on a regular basis? Meaning that over periods of months and years, your body creates new cells for every organ and bone in your body. So, you create a new heart, liver, kidneys, lungs, skeleton, all of it, just as you create new skin, nails, and hair cells. So you ask, "Why then, if someone has, say, liver cancer, why doesn't their body create new healthy liver cells?" Great question. The answer is as long as the person's attitude and energy remain the same, the body continues to produce biochemistry as a result of their emotions and environment that disallows the optimal regeneration of those cells. The stress response halts optimal reproduction because the body's chemistry is in fight, flight, or freeze. In other words, the chemicals produced by stress disallow the body to produce healthy cells. Instead, the body produces cells that are a vibrational match to the field of the body-mind.

*Get your journal and write your answers to the following questions: What is my dominant emotion? How do I feel most of the time? Am I okay with this answer? Would I like to raise my emotional set point? How would I like to feel most of the time? What thoughts do I have to think in order to feel that way? What thoughts am I thinking regularly that I do not want to think any longer?

The key is to remember you are always in charge of how you think and, thus, how you feel. I know it's very difficult sometimes to think and feel greater than your environment. But that is mental and emotional mastery (Samurai style), and it will launch you into the environment that you love in time. Overcome any limiting environments through your thoughts. We will talk more about this in Chapter 3, Unconditional Forgiveness. This is one of your superpowers: the power to think the way you choose. It's a good one!

> This is one of your superpowers: the power to think the way you choose.

By the way, share this powerful information with your parents! It will keep them healthy and happy!

The energy emitted from you as you practice unconditional self-love is a highly attractive magnetic field. Part of loving yourself unconditionally is owning your darkness and not feeling less about yourself because there are areas of you that are wounded or messy, fearful or mad, or just not on board with whatever is going on in front of you at the moment.

> The energy emitted from you as you practice unconditional self-love is a highly attractive magnetic field.

*Ponder the idea of owning yourself in all areas of your life. Own your budding sexuality and sexual expression.

Own your ideas, own your choices, own your mistakes, own your magic, own your power, own your weirdness, own your introverted qualities, and own your extroverted qualities and uniqueness. Own your work-in-progress-ness. The truth is we are all a work in progress, and anyone who isn't is no longer developing themselves, and that is when life gets depressing. Those who "have it all" know their success is because they keep seeking to learn and grow into greater versions of themselves, so no worries if, at times, you feel like you don't know who you are yet. The idea of life is to keep growing and discovering the hidden gems of your genius. Adults who aren't doing that are bored and perhaps slightly miserable.

*Write down the ways you will own yourself that make you feel empowered. Feel yourself embodying this for at least five minutes, then write down any insights that came to you. For instance, choose to own that you already possess the power within you to create whatever you want in life and that the seeds of greatness are indeed within you. Then, close your eyes, take a deep breath, and FEEL what that feels like. Embody that truth. How does it feel? Write it down.

For many of us, it's hard to FEEL powerful because, by the nature of being a kid, perhaps you haven't been allowed to be powerful. You've had others steering your ship, and that has had many benefits for you up until this point. Parents are meant to steer and guide for a time, but it's important that you have an opportunity to feel that you can steer your own ship into your promised land before you step out and do it. And you can. Mental rehearsal is a master key to greatness and living a life experience you love. We will talk in detail about that in Chapter 2. But for now, I want you to use mental rehearsal to feel yourself in command of your life. FEEL yourself capable and responsible for your life experience in a way that excites you.

> Mental rehearsal is a master key to greatness and living a life experience you love.

Here's the thing: learning to consciously create your life experience is fun, and it starts with unconditional self-love. From unconditional self-love, everything blooms, and everything is possible. From unconditional self-love, you become magnetic to the energetic match of unconditional love, which puts you in the flow of life. You are unconditionally loved by the world, by your creator, and by your parents and grandparents, although I know sometimes it might not feel like it. When you establish your energetic set point with strong self-love and respect, you become a match to God's/the Universe's love for you, and life becomes magical.

It's when we are judging ourselves or are destructive with ourselves that the world reflects that, and we suffer. Now I understand that for some, their upbringing has not felt like unconditional love, and worst still, abuse and neglect happen more often than anyone wants to think about. But the best news ever is that regardless of where we started out, we can always create a life we love now and as adults. A life you love is always accessible to you, and this comes from a sense of peace and gratitude for who you are and what you are. You are a creator, designed to create. The basis of your power to create what you actually want in life stems from your foundation of unconditional self-love.

> It's when we are judging ourselves or are destructive with ourselves that the world reflects that, and we suffer.

> A life you love is always accessible to you, and this comes from a sense of peace and gratitude for who you are and what you are.

My amazing media coach, Susie Moore, is so joyful and exuberant in the most genuine way. She is wildly successful in many areas; she's a life coach, media mogul, entrepreneur, and writer who's been featured in every prominent media outlet you can think of. She mentions her upbringing now and again in passing or to give context to someone she's helping. She's a beautiful example of how someone can grow up in and out of domestic violence shelters and lose a parent to addiction at a young age and still create a beautiful life they love. And thank God for her owning herself and her gifts and owning her ability to create a life she loves regardless of circumstance because she has literally changed the lives of tens of thousands of people with her nourishing information and expertise. Just think, how many people might you serve in the future simply by being you and following your own guidance? I'll close out this paragraph with one of my favorite Susie Moore-isms, "Let it be easy." More on creating the neural programming for that in Chapter 2.

The Practices

Let's talk about some practical ways to implement unconditional self-love. There are many exercises you can do to help build those neural pathways. They are fun and will immediately raise your energy and the frequency you are functioning from.

1: <u>Mirror Work.</u> Yes, this might sound hokey, and you can giggle; giggling is always good (unless you're in a quiet church service or something), but it's powerfully effective, and I find it quite fun. Sit or stand in front of a mirror, look yourself in the eyes, and say aloud, "I deeply and completely love and accept myself." Repeat this several times and allow emotions to come through. You may feel awkward at first, but do this alone. No one is watching or judging you. You are free to connect to yourself and feel the deep love and appreciation for your being. Allow this to be your private me-time. Spend at least ten minutes looking at yourself and feeling this love and appreciation. New awareness will come from this practice that radically enhances your life.

Another way you can utilize a mirror is to sit comfortably on the ground in front of a wall mirror, if you have one. Sit in a seated, crossed-legged position in meditation.

The meditation is to look into your eyes while softly repeating and feeling the words "I AM." The idea is to feel yourself as the divine energy that you are. The Bible says, "You are made in the image and likeness of God." What does that mean? It means You are a creator. So look yourself in the eyes and heart and say with certainty, "I AM." And just feel what comes forward. You can say, "I am love,

I am powerful, I am peaceful, I am God." Yes, I said it. You ARE God. We all are. We experience life aligned with this level of ease and flow when we clearly identify ourselves as creators. A word of caution: this exercise is to allow for the greatest versions of yourself to show up and make themselves known in your energy, body, and consciousness. You will feel what it feels like to be what you are declaring. This is not the place to get the "I am mad" out of your system unless you need that, but that's a different exercise. This exercise is to just sit with your higher self, look it in the mirror, and become acquainted with the beauty, good, and loving power that's within you.

> This exercise is to just sit with your higher self, look it in the mirror, and become acquainted with the beauty, good, and loving power that's within you.

2: <u>Cultivate emotional mastery throughout your day.</u> That sounds fun, doesn't it? It is! This means you are mindful of your emotions and triggers and aim to forgive quickly. It means you practice choosing your emotions independent of circumstance. For instance, if you have plenty of reasons to feel lack or victimhood, instead, you choose to feel blessed to be alive and able to learn new ideas. You trust you will arrive at a place in life you love. It's not easy to trust that at times, but yet you do. You practice it consciously because it feels better to be in the higher frequency of faith and expectancy than in victimhood, guilt, or anger. Cultivating emotional mastery takes time and practice. It's something that is truly cultivated only from constantly overcoming your environment and your emotional impulses to rewire new impulses and responses to triggers in your environment. This is awesome to experience. It doesn't take long to rewire responses, and soon, you will be witnessing yourself in more peace, creativity, and acceptance than ever before, and that feels wonderful. Starting this practice as a teenager means you will avoid years, perhaps decades, of misused and misguided energy because you will have wired in higher consciousness before adulthood.

> It means you practice choosing your emotions independent of circumstance.

> Starting this practice as a teenager means you will avoid years, perhaps decades, of misused and misguided energy because you will have wired in higher consciousness before adulthood.

Emotional mastery is a superpower you can possess with practice that many adults have never achieved. I know many adults who let circumstances choose how they feel instead of choosing how they feel based on how they want to feel. What a novel thought, right? How do you want to feel? Guess what, you can decide to feel that and spend time cultivating that feeling so that it's easier to feel. Once you spend time consciously creating the feeling, the neural pathways for those feelings of confidence, peace, joy, wealth, or whatever you want start to get stronger. The more you practice, the stronger they get until that is just who you are unconsciously. We will talk much more about that in Chapter 2.

> Emotional mastery is a superpower you can possess with practice that many adults have never achieved.

If it is hard to FEEL the feelings you want to feel at first, I get it. There were years of my life that metaphysically, I knew I needed to feel prosperous, but life could make me feel the opposite if I wasn't conscious of the power of my feelings. It takes practice to become conscious of your feelings and to choose to take them to the next level. We are not here to ho-hum around in low-grade depression, and we don't have to be excited every moment, either. That might be exhausting. We want to feel centered in peace, knowing we are creators, able to create what our hearts and souls are making known to us through our desires and talents. When we center our emotional set point around this awareness, we are naturally happier and able to roll with life.

> We want to feel centered in peace, knowing we are creators, able to create what our hearts and souls are making known to us through our desires and talents.

Another opportunity to cultivate emotional mastery is when you get in a disagreement with a friend or family member or when you read a comment on social media that triggers you. This is a brilliant opportunity to choose your feelings. To be clear, choosing your feelings doesn't mean to be numb about things; it doesn't mean choosing not to feel. Choosing your feelings in this case looks like, *Okay, me and this person I care about disagree, that's okay. We don't have to agree on everything. They think what they think because of their subconscious mind and experiences, and I think what I think because of my subconscious mind and experiences, so I'll just let them be them, and I'm going to be me. I'm sure this will blow over with love, and if it doesn't, that's okay too. I trust that the people who are for my highest good will be around me, and those who are not for my highest good will drift away. I choose forgiveness, but I also choose to respect myself and not let others have the gift of my friendship and presence if I feel in any way bullied or disrespected.*

In the case of a triggering social media comment, please always adopt the position of WHO CARES. Who cares what they think? Never allow someone, especially someone you don't know, to hurt your feelings. If you are a celebrity or plan to be a celebrity, this is must-have information.

I recently saw an Instagram post from Jojo Siwa, whom I absolutely adore. I could write a book on how amazing I think she is. As someone who is twice her age (maybe more), I think she has always handled her fame with such maturity and grace. I love the empowering messages in her songs. I have two little kids that enjoy a "morning dance party" every morning to her video playlist on YouTube. This is how I got acquainted with Jojo Siwa. It was nice to have music with a positive message instead of all those kids' music videos about sibling rivalry and boys against girls BS. I love that the reason she is so successful is because she is authentically herself. She went for it, it blew up like crazy in all the best ways, and she rode that wave with complete grace, being loyal to herself, her family, her team, and her dancers all along. Fame at that level as a child is not easy; it comes with a very big price. If you don't have the "thick skin" for it, it can take you down, as we've seen happen to many famous people. I recently thought to follow her on Instagram and was looking at some photos she had posted recently. I saw this amazing photo of her styled as a guy. I thought it was interesting, so I clicked on the photo. The first comment I saw was someone giving her opinion, and let's just say it wasn't supportive. I replied to that person with something like, "Why do you think Jojo needs to be who you think she should be? Why would Jojo care what you think of her? She doesn't know you. She can dress and be however she wants. You think she should always be rainbows and sparkles like she was when she was a child?" Or something. I couldn't read any more comments after that. I didn't have time to correct anyone else. LOL! I think I may have felt more momentarily triggered reading that comment on Jojo's page than anything I've read on my own socials. People should never be shamed for expressing themselves how they want to express themselves. We must respect people and acknowledge that every single person has the divine right of self- expression. In fact, every person's true nature is a divine expression.

> In fact, every person's true nature is a divine expression.

My point in sharing that is this: people say stupid things at times. They just do, am I right? Most people are wonderful people, thank God. We can safely say that most people are not a-holes, BUT the tiny percentage that are will find you and post on your socials the moment you put yourself out there to be commented on. The attitude to take is, *That's what you think, but do I care what you think? Do I even know you? Do I like what I posted, and do I like what I have to share?* If so, then, *Sorry, not sorry, but I do not care what you think.* And then never think of it again. Remember, unsupportive opinions from people you don't know don't matter.

This is not to say that you can't learn from others' comments, but there is a difference between constructive criticism and someone just being rude. For instance, I had a show on Hulu called *Blythe Raw Live*. It was a healthy lifestyle show. Clips from that show are on YouTube, and it streamed live to Ustream (back in the day). I got comments about how gross it was that I would touch my hair and then touch food. I wore my hair down (because I had to look good, LOL), but when I looked down to chop vegetables or stir my cacao salt scrub together, my hair would fall in my face, and I had to move it. I was unaware of how "gross" this was for people to see me touch my hair and then touch food. I mean, I wasn't serving them the food, but their comments made me conscious of it. And they were right. It is kind of gross to watch me toss back my hair and then touch coconut meat to put it in the blender. It's not "actually" gross because my hair isn't covered in maggots or filth of some sort. I don't think I'm transferring anything crazy into the food, but in the context of food preparation, hair touching (at least on TV) is incorrect. Their comments helped me show up better. So, we *can* learn from the a-holes sometimes.

Also, while I have you on social media triggers, it may be the best idea ever to bounce off all socials for a time. Bounce off video games for a time and hang with real friends in real life. Go to the park, bat some balls, take a walk to get an ice cream, take a jog with friends, or build something epic with Legos, wooden blocks, or magnetic titles. You're like, uhh, I'm a teenager… but come on, tell me you don't love creating amazing, colorful creations. I love magnetic tiles and wooden blocks. I love how the light comes through the brightly colored transparent tiles and the magnetic click when placed together. I love how colorful wooden blocks look and feel in my hands. I love being able to create something colorful that then gets put away instead of filling my house more with artwork. I am an artist, and I love to paint, but if I paint every day, my house becomes encumbered with canvases. There's something to be said for being creative in fun ways that don't leave something behind. So I encourage you to build, play, and create in real life, with real people. This will naturally help keep you feeling good and able to master your emotions. Did you know that expressing yourself creatively in any way, from freestyle rapping to freestyle writing, singing, dancing, painting, or playing as suggested above or any other way you desire, for at least twenty minutes a day, will shape your brain in new ways? These new neural pathways strengthen your identity and give you the confidence to follow through on opportunities that come your way. For instance, say you love to sing but feel like you would never be able to sing your heart out in front of people and definitely never impromptu. If you sang for the love of singing every day for at least twenty minutes, you would create the identity of someone who sings. You would recognize and magnetize opportunities to sing. When an opportunity to sing in front of people presents itself, say karaoke at a party, or the lead singer of a local band you love bails, and they need someone quick, you can step into that opportunity with confidence because you've practiced, and you've built the neural pathways to make singing a part of your identity. You're probably thinking, *I've done this before many times, like from my bedroom*, but singing is the same in your bedroom or in a venue. You'll start to think, *I've got this.*

3: <u>Self-Love Meditation</u>. I have recorded a self-love meditation session for you. You can listen at BlytheNaturalLiving.com/selflovemeditation.

*Grab a journal and write down what unconditional self-love means to you. How might you show yourself unconditional self-love? Write your thoughts on that, just stream of thought, don't edit yourself, and enjoy the process.

Another incredible benefit to practicing unconditional self-love is it automatically makes you more loving and accepting of others. When you come from a place of self-love, you are a lot less judgmental and critical of others, which just feels better. You don't have an interest in gossip or pointing out other people's faults. You literally are on a higher wavelength, above the consciousness of judgment. This is an amazing place to be. Imagine if you didn't have ill feelings toward others, even when perhaps their behavior merits it. Seeing the love and beauty in everyone changes your life. It makes you more open to possibilities that come through people that you may not have otherwise seen. It diminishes walls you put up as protection because unconditional self-love is protection. You don't need to worry about others hurting you because you don't let them. In fact, your energy of unconditional self-love sends out a powerful signal that others pick up on, and it changes how they treat you. Talk about a superpower.

> Seeing the love and beauty in everyone changes your life.

> Your energy of unconditional self-love sends out a powerful signal that others pick up on, and it changes how they treat you.

If there is someone in your life who is not treating you well, turn up your unconditional self-love and watch how that changes the dynamic of the relationship. People will either rise to your level or fall out of your life, temporarily or permanently. In relation to your parents, watch how your practice of unconditional self-love improves how they relate to you. Speaking as a mother of two young children, I can say that most of the time, when parents are trying to exert control over their children, it's to protect them (or so they think). Your parents will feel shifts in you, and they will sense you are stronger and more confident. They will sense your love for yourself. They won't know why, but they will trust you to make good choices, which will relinquish their need for control. Whether they pick up on it consciously or subconsciously, you will experience positive upgrades in that relationship by practicing unconditional self-love.

Your Fantastic Immunity

I'm referring to immunity in two ways here. Immunity is our body's intricate and outstanding defense system against pathogens, which keeps us healthy and alive. AND it's our immunity from outside influence when we choose it. In other words, "I don't give a f**k." I mean this in the best possible way. I mean this in the sense that when you know something in your heart and when something resonates with you, what others think or say doesn't touch you. Immunity, in this sense, means that you are immune to criticism if it's not something you can learn from. You are immune to other's ridicule; why should what they think bother you? This kind of immunity comes with being strong on the inside but in a graceful way. You don't have to be hard to be strong. True inner strength is knowing you are enough, right now, right here. Both kinds of immunity are strengthened with unconditional self-love.

> True inner strength is knowing you are enough, right now, right here.

Our body's physical immune system exists in our glands, our skin, our bones, and our blood. The teeny tiny sparks of life that exist as our cells telepathically communicate with each other in a fantastic symphony called the immune response. How amazing are you?! VERY!

The immune system isn't just one bodily response, like creating antibodies to overcome pathogens; it's many responses happening all at once. All these amazing responses happen automatically without you having to think about them. Talk about a genius program. And all these responses are made stronger through unconditional self-love.

Many studies have been conducted that show the relationship between self-love and health. I recall one such study conducted by Dr. Joe Dispenza's team, where they measured the immunoglobulin A (IgA) of participants before and after a four-day meditation retreat. Their study found their participants' immune response improved by greater than 50 percent. This is outstanding evidence. You literally up-level your physical immune strength by living in a place of peace and love. In this study, the participants created what is called brain and heart coherence, where you sit in stillness and release all identities, as Dr. Joe guided them to become "no person, in no time, in no place." He then guided them to put their attention on the endless space that exists around them and around our planet Earth. There really is endless space. Isn't that an amazing thing to contemplate? You can enjoy many of his meditations on YouTube.

Sitting and truly contemplating endless space, and allowing yourself to dissolve into endless space, creates this brain and heart coherence that completely shifts your life if you let it. Let's be honest: it's not always easy to sit your body and mind down for a time to explore space inside your consciousness. A downfall of the digital age is that there is always something shiny to look at that takes your attention away from your own genius. This is precisely why the CDC says that 70 percent of teenagers struggle with depression and anxiety. A person will feel depressed and anxious if their attention is always on the outside world and never on the inside. If there is a device in our pocket that is always summoning us to look at it, our neural pathways are so ingrained to be constantly looking at it. This means we are automatically looking at our phones, going through the apps we check routinely, and never having the time to check in with our own genius. Our own genius gets trumped by the noise of social media and others' expectations. It's no wonder people feel depressed in these conditions. However, you have a choice. You can choose to check in with yourself before you check in with anything on your phone. Once you make that choice repeatedly, you will create neural wiring to check in with yourself first. Checking in with yourself means remembering what you want to create; this puts your focus on your end results. We'll talk more about that in Chapter 2.

> Our own genius gets trumped by the noise of social media and others' expectations. It's no wonder people feel depressed in these conditions.

It only takes a choice to put away your device and sit quietly with yourself to allow new levels of yourself to come through. It takes consistent choice. Just like creating anything amazing takes consistent practice and commitment. The only way to find yourself is to spend time with yourself. Let this be fun. The good news is, anytime you are sitting and attempting to connect to yourself, to your higher self, to God, to the Universe, to your angels, to your guides, to the quantum field, Source energy, or whatever you want to call it, you are blessing your body with a treatment. The treatment is creating that brain and heart coherence that alkalizes the body, and that creates biochemistry that heals and regenerates the body. So many good things are happening when you take time to sit, envision, and connect with Source energy. You will get ideas, you will get guidance, and you will feel the love that the world has for you. Because, my Dear Teenager, the world loves you and needs you. You have a special genius that only you have.

There is a gift inside you that the world will benefit from. Your job is to let that happen by following your natural talents and desires and believing in your gifts and yourself.

> The only way to find yourself is to spend time with yourself. Let this be fun.

> There is a gift inside you that the world will benefit from. Your job is to let that happen by following your natural talents and desires and believing in your gifts and yourself.

A practice such as that improves your immunity in both senses of the word. It not only creates a stronger physical immune system in your body, but it also creates a stronger immunity to the world's troubles and the constant chaos that is available to stress about if we let ourselves. You don't need to take on the weight of the world. Like the kid I mentioned earlier, who drove his car off an overpass on purpose because he felt that life wasn't worth living based on listening to the news on current affairs. He walked away from that experience, hopefully realizing that something beyond physics and reason saved him that day. His genius was meant to have a greater expression, and Life kept him here to have that expression.

Immunity to criticism is a wonderful thing. I'm sure there will be people who will criticize this book. Maybe there will be something I can learn there, or maybe the remarks won't resonate with me, which means they aren't for me, so why should I engage with the remarks emotionally? Do you see how building my unconditional self-love and building my connection with Source/God/quantum field allows me to take actions that I couldn't take if I were worried about what others thought? Do you see how you might stop yourself from expressing yourself in some way based on fear of others' responses?

We do that because, as babies, toddlers, and young children, we have been taught to comply. We have been taught and perhaps punished for not following other peoples' rules. It creates fear of upsetting others or going against the grain. We feel our belonging is threatened if we don't behave as required. Compliance and conformity are required in many school environments and celebrated. I understand that some rules are necessary for structure in schools and society, so there is logic and reason as to why schools are set up this way. However, we forget to teach children to be themselves while following the rules of school and home environments.

For children, when they express something that is uniquely theirs, and it doesn't go over well with family or teachers, they feel their "belonging" has been threatened. So they unconsciously train that authenticity out of them for fear of not belonging. Some parents are better than others at embracing their children for who they are and not who the parent expects them to be.

At the time of writing this book, I have an eight-year-old daughter and a four-year-old son. I have visions of us dancing together, meditating together, doing our daily visioning together. However, they are not into it, not yet anyway. They love to dance, but they don't want to learn choreography and create a dance that we can rock out together. This is something I would love to do on a regular basis for fitness, creativity, and fun time with them. It checks three boxes at once! But alas, they are not into it at this time. I am a martial artist, and my daughter has let me teach her the blocks and strikes with a Bo staff, but she refuses to train with me in a safe way; she just wants to go bananas with her staff. As much as I love to play Wonder Woman to her Super Girl in the backyard, she doesn't yet have the maturity to train safely, so we just can't. As much as I wish I could interact with my kids in ways that are fun for me, I want to meet them where they are. So, I resound, for now, to playing magical creature society in the bedroom with the plush unicorns and other assorted magical creature cuddle toys during our playtime together. Which *is* fun, but it just means I must find another time to exercise because Mama needs a workout! I can see how parents who like certain sports want their kids to play that sport or have similar interests because it's fun to do together. I think it's important that parents share their interests and talents with their kids and invite them into it. But it's more important that our children feel free to find their true individuality while feeling totally supported in doing so. Would you agree? Just for fun, take a few minutes and think about what kinds of activities you'd like to do with your parents or family. Perhaps bring this up to your family. You may just start a new family tradition.

In Chapter 3, you will learn about how to forgive and forget everything that kept you small or kept you from expressing your genius. You have the power in the Now moment to create the version of yourself that makes you feel so good. The version of yourself that is aligned with your destiny. It's a good place to be, and it is something that is always growing and flowing. It's not like you arrive at alignment, and that's it. You will be becoming grander versions of yourself for your entire life. But you will always be where you need to be at the right time. Getting in touch with what resonates with you creates clarity and certainty. That clarity and certainty allow you to be immune to the opinions of others and seek your own guidance.

> You have the power in the Now moment to create the version of yourself that makes you feel so good.

Others can and will be a huge help to you in accomplishing whatever you set out to do, so please don't misunderstand the message. Other people are key to your happiness and fulfillment, but not everyone will be. Discerning what opinions or feedback will benefit you is as easy as taking a moment to be still with yourself and see if the feedback resonates in your body. How does your body *feel* physically when you receive that feedback or that opinion? Let me teach you a simple, intuitive feedback exercise you can do to know if something is right for you.

Intuition Exercise: Feeling a Yes and a No

Think about a time in your life when you absolutely knew something was right for you. Feel what that Yes feeling feels like in your body. Notice the actual FEELings. Is there a tingle sensation? Is there a warm sensation or a cold sensation? Do you feel it in your heart, your gut, or somewhere else? Where do you feel this Yes feeling? Notice this and then bring up another time when you knew something was right for you. Do you get the same physical sensation? This is your Yes feeling. Now, bring up a time when something was not right for you, where something was definitely wrong for you, and it was a No. Notice what this No feeling feels like. Where in your body do you feel it? What characterizes the feeling? Does it feel heavy or dark or hot? Now, bring up another time you know that something was absolutely not right for you. Does it feel the same way in your body when you think of it? This is your No feeling.

In reference to what is mentioned in the paragraph right before the intuition exercise about knowing if certain feedback or people are right for you, use this exercise to feel if the feedback, situation, or person is right for you. Notice if the physical feeling is associated with the Yes feeling, or does it feel more like a No feeling? Can you discern what is meant to serve you and what is just noise through how it makes your body feel? If you practice connecting with yourself and with information in this way, you will create absolute knowing. This will benefit you in every way.

I was watching *Jennifer Lopez: Halftime*, a documentary on Netflix about J.Lo's experience leading up to her performance at the 2020 Super Bowl. There's a scene where she's in a large dressing area with racks of gowns on either side of her. She is trying them on and deciding which one she wants to wear to an award show for her film *Hustlers*. As I watched her stand on her dressing platform with her team around her in these gorgeous gowns, I thought, *That's not allowed*. I had a brief subconscious thread of thoughts that I became aware of that said, *That's frivolous; you're not allowed to be the center of attention. It's wrong to be the center of attention with everyone concerned about you looking perfect. It's frivolous to be so concerned with beauty.* It was like I thought it was "wrong" to put so much emphasis on beauty and fashion and "wrong" to be a star garnering all the attention. Split-second thinking. I recognized these quick thoughts that ran through my consciousness because I knew they didn't belong to me. That's not how I feel at all. I love fashion. I'm so grateful for art, fashion, and luxury because without it, life would be bland. What if everything in life was just for survival? Plenty of people have lived that experience historically, and we've evolved out of it because humans are meant to express art and fashion and music and movies. This adds so much to life. I became aware that I had subconscious programming from childhood that said, "I'm not allowed to have that. I'm not allowed to be the center of attention." That wasn't *my* voice, it was my mother's voice. My mother wasn't into luxury and glamour; that was frivolous to her and, therefore, inappropriate. I also think growing up in a family with four kids, I wasn't really allowed to be special. It wasn't appropriate that I stand out. At least, that's how I felt. The feeling was, "Who do you think you are to want a fantasy dress or fancy experiences?" It wasn't allowed. My mom did buy my sisters and me dresses for school dances like Homecoming and Prom, so it's not as though I was deprived of wearing nice dresses on occasion, but what I'm talking about here is the sense that luxury and stardom felt inappropriate to want. Like it was not allowed. So, if I desire to be a dolled-up star, that threatens my sense of belonging to my family. All that lay dormant in my subconscious, running my life, until I had the experience of recognizing that I was thinking thoughts that were not mine.

This programming runs deep. It's not to blame our parents that I bring this up, but to make us aware of what truth belongs to us and what "truths" have been passed down that don't resonate with us at all. Some of these beliefs that get passed down don't even resonate with our parents, but they never recognized them or believed they were allowed to live any differently.

J.Lo said something truly profound in the documentary. Sitting around a long table full of family and friends with a beautiful holiday feast awaiting them, she takes a moment to acknowledge her parents for the tremendous part they played in her massive success. She said, "My parents always told me I could be anything. They taught me to believe in my dreams and go after them." This was the programming she received. This is what her subconscious mind took as the truth. So as J.Lo went out in life and came across failures and struggles early in her career, her underlying belief was, *I can do anything, and I will.* This belief has served her tremendously well. This belief allowed her subconscious mind not to create blocks when failures happened, allowing her to keep going. The belief also gave her a posture and presence of *I can do this*, even when her conscious mind was struggling with insecurities.

After hearing her express gratitude to her parents, I thought about whether I had received messages like that in childhood. After giving it some thought, I realized I was never told, "You can be anything you want" or "Follow your talents and dreams." I feel like the dominant impression I had from childhood was, "I'm not allowed to have what I want, so stop asking!" Growing up in a family of four kids with a single, blue-collar income, there was an economic reason for this position, I'm sure. However, J.Lo grew up in a one-bedroom apartment with a family of five. Even though

J.Lo's parents couldn't give her everything she wanted as a child, they still instilled in her that SHE could create what she wanted in her life. They instilled in her her own power. This was her foundation, and she built an empire on it. And so can you.

For me, I had to teach myself this. I am so grateful I had the audacity to follow my own soul as a teenager and to this day. I have created wonderful things, and I've had many failures. I would create seven-figure opportunities for myself, and they would fall apart. I had so many amazing "Yeses" that somehow didn't turn into the mega success I assumed they would. It wasn't until I studied the subconscious mind that I understood why this was happening. My subconscious mind was trained from ages zero to seven. It was trained in how to stay safe in the world. In childhood, staying safe means belonging. We must feel a belonging to our family. Everything I was trying to create with my conscious mind was being sabotaged by my subconscious mind because it threatened my belonging. As an adult, this makes no sense. My family would not dislike me if I became a superstar. On the contrary, I'm sure they would be quite proud of me, excited for me, and certainly happy that I'm treating us all to Hawaiian vacations. But the subconscious is just that, sub-conscious. I had no conscious awareness that I was sabotaging myself. My subconscious would step in and say, in essence, *No, this isn't our identity; this identity threatens belonging. It can't happen*. Then, the block in consciousness disallows right-action and collapses a reality aligned with the old familiar identity. I was on that loop for a while until I committed to the practices I teach you in this book. Doing the practices from this book daily will wire your subconscious mind for the identity you choose instead of the one your environment has dictated for you. Doing the exercises teaches your subconscious mind that you are already that identity. It's a powerful thing.

The J.Lo documentary was truly inspiring in so many ways. She's just a girl like any of us. She listened to her talents and desires, and it led her to superstardom. But it wasn't easy, and it didn't come without a lot of criticism. She endured the most ridiculous media criticism. I remember back in the day when her star was rising (before you were born), the media kept talking about her butt. I mean, really media? That's just stupid, isn't it? We don't realize how hard she worked and how much she had to believe in herself when no one else did. When Hollywood executives would dismiss her for being Latino, she had to ignore them and instead believe in her talent and passion. Even after she was a star, she said she had such low self-esteem because the media kept criticizing her talent, her body, and her choices. However, because she did have a sense of unconditional self-love, she stayed after it. She is enjoying new levels of self-discovery and success because she didn't let the criticism take her down. She didn't listen to Hollywood when it said, "You can either be a dancer or an actress or a pop star." She said, "No, I can do all the things." And she did, with legendary success.

So, my Dear Teenager, let me leave you with these questions as we close this chapter together: What can your unconditional self-love create in your life? How might practicing unconditional self-love improve your immediate environment? Then, just do it, keep doing it, and watch what happens and keeps happening. Life will feel more beautiful in every way. Like a force field, your unconditional self-love will shield and protect you, and like a radio antenna (what's that? LOL), it will put out a frequency that draws to you circumstances that match it. It's good stuff.

Chapter 2
2nd Key
Imagineering ~ The Art of Conscious Creation

Oh, I love this topic! Get ready; you are about to discover an inner technology that is foundational in creating a life you love in every way. Imagineering is the idea that we embody in consciousness first what we want to create in form. What we focus on with elevated emotion, through our vision and intention (imagination), becomes our life experience. It's not a passive activity of thinking and waiting for your miracles, it's an active protocol in consciousness that includes directing and cultivating elevated emotions in response to images and scenes conquered. I will walk you through the process in this chapter, so no worries if you have no idea what I'm talking about. I take you step by step through the process later in the chapter.

Reggie Jackson talks about how he spent his entire youth envisioning he was a professional basketball player. He felt it over and over and over again. Every day. He sat and visioned himself in that life, playing ball. He *felt* himself playing professional basketball. His result? He was offered an eighty-million- dollar contract at age twenty-five. Pretty awesome! The world over is full of these stories of those who dared to dream. But it's more than dreaming; it's even more than believing. It's knowing, having unwavering faith and knowingness in the vision, regardless of present-day circumstances.

I would say that every single professional athlete saw themselves as a professional athlete. They practiced hard and held a vision and belief that they could get there. I don't think any professional athlete is surprised they got there; no one is saying, "I don't know how this happened, it just happened." They know exactly how it happened. They believed it could happen. That belief caused the action to train hard to be the best. That belief caused them not to give up when it got hard. By believing they could do it, they set in motion the circumstances for scouts to recognize them and for their talent to unfold in bigger ways.

I have experienced many times how my focus and attention directly affected outcomes in my life. When I was eighteen years old, I was diagnosed with a hideous virus. I was told I would have it my entire life, and there was nothing I could do about it. I could take drugs if I wanted, but that wouldn't "heal" it or even ensure no symptoms. I just said, "No." I never entertained the thought of having to deal with something horrible in my health for the rest of my life. I definitely wasn't about to take ongoing medication. I refused it. As a result, it did not exist for me. I don't know how I knew to be so bold at eighteen years old, but I had no doubt. I would not live a life with any kind of health problem. My certainty made it so. But not just my certainty, my certainty paired with my unconditional self-love. Knowing and Love are a power couple.

> Knowing and Love are a power couple.

The experience made me inquire and study about my own self-healing design. What I've learned about the power we have in creating thriving health through our consciousness needs to be known and understood in our culture. I have never had any indication of that virus in almost thirty years. It doesn't exist for me. I said, "No."

In my early twenties, I was acting in a small Lion's Gate film. We were shooting overnight in the woods in Big Bear, California. It was around five a.m., the end of the first of four nights in the woods, where I was to be running from danger and obstacles, when I tripped and fell. I heard and felt a snap. My ankle swelled up immediately, black and blue, and it hurt so bad. I cried. That was a wrap for the day. The set medic wrapped it and did what she could. I was asked a few times if I wanted to go to the emergency room, but I declined. I knew that if I went to the emergency room, I was putting the entire production at risk. I was carried to a vehicle that took me back to the house that was rented for the cast. I was carried into bed. I laid there, remembering literally the first thing I was ever taught in acting class: "Actors don't get sick." There are a lot of people who work on a production, and a lot of money is spent each day. It's very unfavorable if it has to stop because a lead actor can't make it. I saw the director's nervous face as I was carried off the set. I knew he was wondering what tomorrow would bring. What would production do, and would he have to scramble to try to shoot something else that day instead of the scheduled running scenes? I know that may not sound like a big pivot, but in filmmaking, shooting off schedule can be nearly impossible.

As I lay in bed in the wee hours of the morning, I said firmly to myself, "I am healed, my ankle is healed." I repeated this over and over, again and again. With knowing. With love. With the acceptance of this miracle, I said, "My ankle is well and good." I saw myself waking up and ready to run. I saw myself miraculously healed. I remember having the thread of consciousness that I was healed throughout the entire night (or day, as it were) that I slept. When I woke up at about three p.m. to make it to set by four for an overnight shoot, my ankle was completely healed. It was not even sore. No discoloration. No trace of the injury from just that morning at five. It was incredible. I felt incredible about it. But I also totally expected that. I would not let a doubt creep into my mind about whether or not my ankle was well. It was well, I declared it so, I believed it, it had to be, and it was.

That was the second time I radically healed something acute, immediately and permanently. I became fascinated with healing, thriving, and biohacking. I REALized (made real for me) the power we have in creating lifelong health and vitality and choosing our longevity. Moreover, the effect our daily thinking and way of being has on our body and health is really good information to have.

I decided to get a Ph.D. in metaphysical sciences to understand the power the mind has in literally creating the body. What I've learned and experienced has shaped my life. I know I can continue to determine thriving health for myself, and that is one of the best freedoms. I want you to have that, too, and that's why I'm writing this book. But it doesn't stop with our physical body; we also shape our environment and circumstances through our conscious focus.

You will have much less pain and suffering in your life when you practice the exercises I teach you in this chapter and in this book. And better still, you will create so much more joy and fulfillment. You will see your creative talents manifest in forms that serve others as well as finance your amazing life. You'll see.

Think about yourself and your life as a 3D print of your consciousness. If you feel disempowered because your parents suck, you hate your teachers and school, and you are disenchanted with the world, your life will print just like that. If you feel self-conscious and unsafe putting yourself out there, your life will print in that way, meaning you will experience that energy more in your life. Conversely, when you start to feel unconditional self-love and unconditional forgiveness (which we'll talk about in Chapter 3), and you start to feel confident in yourself, your life will "print" opportunities to express that confidence.

> Think about yourself and your life as a 3D print of your consciousness.

This is where it gets really fun because it puts you in the driver's seat for the exciting ride of your life. Perhaps it seemed your parents were in the driver's seat, or your perceptions of the world, or the misguided haters that just hate because they haven't been taught that love is much more powerful than hate. Where it seemed like those things were driving forces, now you can relax into the knowing that your consciousness is King or Queen. Your consciousness is really calling the shots. This chapter will help you understand your consciousness as your mighty tool for crafting life experiences that bring you joy and purpose.

When I was a freshman in high school, the senior girls decided to hate me because the senior boys liked me, and the senior girls did not like that. So they took every chance to cackle meanness at me, write my name with profanity on desks, and just be lame jerks. Had I had the understanding then that they were revealing their own insecurity in their behavior, I could have made it clear what was really happening. If the bully knows that everyone knows that "bully" behavior is really just insecurity, a need to put others down to make oneself feel stronger, the whole concept of bullying would be gone. The jig is up! We all know that the bully reveals themself as insecure, and no bully wants to do that.

I share that story with you so you know that I understand the social dynamics that sometimes come into play in the teenage years. When I watch my eight-year-old on the playground, the kids are sweet and inclusive, and everyone plays together. Wouldn't it be nice if that was your experience in high school?

*Ponder what it would feel like to go to school in an environment where everyone knows that being kind and supportive of every single person is really the cool thing. Where everyone knows that being kind allows every student to step into greatness.

> Being kind allows every student to step into greatness.

*Write down the following question and answer it in your journal: What are five things that would make school a better place to be? What are five things that would make home a better place to be? How can I help make these happen?

Imagineering ~ Time to get creative and focus

Focus ~ who's got it? Right! We are bombarded with distractions or potential distractions all day long. Focus is something we must command of ourselves. We have to be intentional about focusing on the things that make us have the life we want. If you want to be better at something, you have to give it time and focus. Our entire lives depend on our ability to focus and learn. Focus means you put 100 percent of your attention on something, and you are present with your entire being. It's awesome how we are capable of multitasking so many things; however, for real learning or manifesting to happen, full attention is required. Creativity is defined as "the use of imagination or original ideas." In Imagineering, we put these two things, creativity and focus, together with the objective of creating the life we want.

Let me explain how to do it, and then I'll explain how it works.

The Ideal Self Exercise

In my Self-Healing Design workshops, I have people create their Ideal Self on paper before creating the blueprint in consciousness. The exercise is to take your notebook and write "<u>Ideal</u> Self" on the top of the page and underline it. This exercise will use five pages of your notebook. On top of the first page, write "Body". On the second page, write "Mind". On the third page, write "Relationships", then "Wealth" on the fourth, and lastly, "Creative Expression" on the fifth page.

On each page, write out aspects of your ideal self in each category. For example, in the "Body" category, you might write things like—create a regular workout, heal my injury, take gymnastics class, get a massage, study martial arts, clear acne, be and feel 100 percent healthy, strengthen my eyesight, heal my PMS, or whatever you would like to create for your body. You want to write things that you can work on, so don't write your ideal height is six-foot-one, but you are five-seven. You want to write down what you can achieve, either through thought or physical effort. In the case of wanting to be a different height, write down—feel totally loving and accepting of my height. This book will show you that you can accomplish a whole lot more with your focused creative thought than you ever knew.

For example, on my "Body" page, I have written—perfect eyesight, lifelong health and vitality, fit body, dance, aerial silk workouts, Pilates, martial arts, swimming in the ocean, playing with my kids, the Tibetan 5 Rites, jumping on the trampoline with my kids, getting my splits back, and having life-changing, full body energy orgasms whenever I want; can I write that in a book for teens? I don't know (eek face). However, I do know that we all benefit from understanding our sexuality from a higher perspective, but that's another book. No need to rush your sexual exploration or expression; you have your whole life for that. This "Body" page is about writing your ideals when it comes to your physical body, many of which you may already be experiencing. It's about getting it on paper. Many things in my Ideal Body list I already experience, so it's not just about writing what you don't have; it's about identifying what you really want from your physical form. Like, I want to dance more. I want to feel super strong and increase the number of pull-ups I can do each month. I want to ice skate. I want to water ski. I want to sign up for a marathon. I want to love and respect my body at all times. Get it? Have fun with this. This is where you create anything you want by writing it down and acknowledging all your preferences. Challenge yourself to learn something new about yourself.

Go about filling in aspects of your Ideal Self in all five categories. Enjoy this process. Write down anything that comes to mind. You can revise it anytime.

Take some time with this exercise. It's fun to ponder all these areas of your life and what you want to create in these areas. On the "Mind" page, write the thoughts you want to think and the emotions you want to feel. This is an incredible exercise to do. It's rewarding and eye-opening to ponder, *What do I want to think throughout my day?* Write down how you want others to feel around you. Write down what you want your dominant mental state to be. So often, with my clients, when I ask them how they want to feel, they are taken aback. They don't realize that they can choose how they want to feel, and they can choose what thoughts they want to think. Believe me, I understand how easy it is to let our environments dictate how we feel (cue the meltdown when I see my four- year-old has spilled half a bag of coffee grounds from the freezer all over the floor in his attempt to find the ice cream I hid in the back of the freezer), but that is not the path to creating a life you love. In my case, if I got annoyed or upset every time my kids made a mess, I would be annoyed every day. I don't want to live like that. If you let your environment dictate how you feel, you will always be a victim of circumstance. But you're not a victim, you are a creator. You are always creating based on where your focus is, so you will create life experiences that you want and that feel good when you focus on the thoughts and feelings that feel good, such as *I am grateful to be learning new things. I am grateful for my talents. I am grateful for my family. This thing I'm dealing with is hard, but I know I will overcome it. This person in my life sucks, but I forgive them because they had a bad childhood and don't know better. I live in total abundance. I have an abundance of life nurturing oxygen to breathe. I have an abundance of healthy food to eat. All my needs are met… etc.* You get the idea. Look for what you want to see. Look for the good, the God, in everything. Observing a single flower can totally wow your mind if you let it. When I plant a seed in the soil and get carrots, that is a miracle. There are miracles surrounding us every minute.Tap into that, and life becomes magical. But you must notice the miracles; you must participate in the magic through your mind. Getting into the habit of looking for the good, the God, that's in everything, will support you in creating a life you love your entire life.

> If you let your environment dictate how you feel, you will always be a victim of circumstance.

> There are miracles surrounding us every minute.Tap into that, and life becomes magical.

In the "Wealth" column, be free to express what you really want in life. What would you like your money set point to be? Meaning, what would you like your baseline income to be now, in your twenties, thirties, forties, and beyond? What kind of life experiences interest you that you can buy with money, such as creating art or music, traveling, starting a business, or giving to others? If you want to travel, decide how much money you want to spend on travel each year. If you want to have homes all over the world and Airbnb them for income, write it down. If you want to be an investor someday and contribute to your community, but you have no idea how that will transpire, write it down. Write down everything that comes to mind, and there is no need to edit your brainstorm of what you want. This is your opportunity to get in touch with your true preferences in life. So often, we don't even realize our true preferences because we are in an environment that disallows them, consciously or unconsciously. This is an opportunity to have total freedom in your financial preferences.

For instance, one thing I've wanted for a long time is to buy a property with many acres of land in California to plant a rainbow orchard. A variety of fruit trees making up the rainbow of colors. Doesn't that sound wonderful? But my desire isn't for me, as my family and I can't eat that much fruit. I want to establish the Los Angeles Free Farmers Market as a non-profit and hire a team to cultivate, harvest, and distribute the organic produce to low-income families in the greater Los Angeles area. Where money is super tight, children are fed non-food (chips, candy, soda, fast food) instead of real food because real food costs more. Kids that eat chips, sodas, and candy on a regular basis instead of real food are much more likely to develop diseases when they get older, sinking their quality of life. This is something I think would be quite valuable for our community, and one day, I'll have the funds to do it. So, this is on my "Wealth" page. Other things on my Wealth page are treating my entire family to amazing vacations and having a sprawling vacation home in Kauai that I use as an income property. This page can have big things and not-so-big things, like getting a massage once a week. You get the idea. Play with this and have fun. What do you want to create that costs money? Go!

On the "Relationships" page, write down how you want your relationship with your parents to feel. Write down how you want your relationships with siblings, friends, and schoolmates to feel. Write down how you want to show up for others. Write down what you want in a significant other(s) when you get there. How do you want to be treated? What do you want people to see in you? These are profound questions to answer. By answering these questions, you help to create the relationships the way you like. Without identifying exactly how you want to feel and show up in relationships, how can you expect to have relationships show up the way you want? You, in part, craft the dynamic of every relationship. By doing this work, you will be consciously crafting the relationship, which means it's much more likely to show up as you like. Of course, there are challenging people that may be placed in your life. Perhaps your parents are challenging, or there are people at school that you don't vibe with. In these cases, choose how you want the relationship to go. You can decide you want to feel a deeper connection with your parents so they trust you more, and you can enjoy more freedom if they trust you more. Just by identifying that you want to have a closer relationship with your parents, you are setting the stage for that to transpire. Getting along with your parents will make your life better in most cases. You may write down that you want to get to know your parents as people. What are their interests besides work and parenting? Your intention to connect with them will shift your dynamic.

> You, in part, craft the dynamic of every relationship.

In the case of people at school who aren't kind or don't resonate with you, you could write, "I see the divine in all and release all judgment of others. I choose to feel at peace with all people. People don't need to be who I think they should be. I choose to release negative feelings toward others when they show up and dissolve those feelings into the knowing that everyone is on their path. I don't need to be friends with anyone who doesn't uplift me. I choose to give my attention to people who inspire me. I choose to see the good in people. I choose not to let anyone take my peace. Nobody can take my joy, as nobody has that power in my life. I choose to contribute my light to others, knowing that light is always coming back to me." Or something along those lines that feels right for you.

On the "Creative Expressions" page, write down how you want to express yourself. This could be artistic expression or not. Creative means to create, so on this page, think about what you want to create in your life now and in the next few years. It could be that you want to create straight As on your report card, or it could mean you want to create time to play music or write music. Maybe you want to create a new club at school for chess or martial arts or something they don't offer, but you know you can take leadership of. Maybe what you want to create is a peaceful and relaxed disposition that helps everyone else relax in your presence. I know a few people like that; they are just so zen that it helps others around them be more zen.

This exercise has two main functions: to get you to put down on paper your ideal expression in the main areas of life and then to use this map in our Imagineering work, which is a closed-eye process I will lead you through shortly.

Imagineering ~ The Practice of Conscious Creation Begins

I've only ever seen the word *Imagineering* used to describe the creative team at Walt Disney. The word means "to implement creative ideas into practical form." And that is exactly what we are going to do, but perhaps in a different way than its definition suggests. We are going to use our imagination, with focus and elevated emotion, to produce form in our lives. This process may or may not produce immediate results, but the results will come.

"Whatever pictures you hold in your mind, the brain translates the picture into complimentary chemistry. The chemistry goes into the blood, the cells adjust their biology by what you perceive in your mind." ~ Bruce Lipton, Biologist, Epigeneticist.

The work Bruce Lipton has done with epigenetics has scientifically proven that our genes are signaled by our environment and consciousness. Genes and DNA are *not* fixed and handed down to us from our lineage like science used to think. Whenever I hear anyone talking about heredity in reference to degenerative diseases, I know they are not abreast of the latest science. However, what is handed down to us from our family and environment are our thought patterns, and it is these thought patterns that create our disease or health, our wealth or lack, and everything in between.

Science has known for a long time that what we think affects our bodies. Medicine knows it too. It's called a placebo; however, they seem to ignore this profound phenomenon. What we think can make us sick and can make us well. But what we think doesn't just affect our physical health, it affects every aspect of our life, our relationships, our finances, and our creative expression, all the areas of our Ideal Selves.

> What we think can make us sick and can make us well. But what we think doesn't just affect our physical health, it affects every aspect of our life, our relationships, our finances, and our creative expression, all the areas of our Ideal Selves.

What are you thinking about most of the day? What energy do you contribute to the space you're in? Become conscious of your running thoughts and emotions throughout your day. Become mindful of the quality of energy that you are emanating and how that's drawing certain experiences to you.

> Become mindful of the quality of energy that you are emanating and how that's drawing certain experiences to you.

The Imagineering meditation exercise I am about to teach you will be more effective when you are conscious of your energy throughout the day. I spent years meditating only to then get up and get annoyed when I had to do the dishes or disappointed that I didn't get the gig or feeling just blah instead of gratitude. It took forever for me to realize that it's not enough to do the work in meditation, you must live the work thereafter. You must take the new you that you created in the Imagineering meditation with you when you wake out of meditation. It's hard at first, I won't lie, and that's why it took me years to figure that piece out. I am a relaxed person, at least I have created myself to be, but I spent way too long getting annoyed about little inconveniences or things not going as I expected. When doing the Imagineering work, expect the unexpected, yet know the end result you want is imminent in time. You want to always be feeling your end results.

> You must take the new you that you created in the Imagineering meditation with you when you wake out of meditation.

Imagineering Meditation Instructions

Sit up tall with your eyes closed. A straight back helps your nervous system relax but keeps you awake. Laying down is fine, too; however, you may fall asleep.

Take several deep breaths; I like to do a six-six breath, which means a six-count inhale and six-count exhale. This puts your brainwaves in a relaxed, open, creative, responsive place.

Next, thank yourself for taking the time and focus to do this work. Thank your body for all the work it does to keep you healthy. The more you thank and appreciate your body, the healthier you will be. How awesome is that, seriously? It turns out our physical tissues are just microorganisms that love to receive gratitude and work better for it, just like anyone else.

> The more you thank and appreciate your body, the healthier you will be.

So, as you are loving up your body and mind, set an intention for this session. The intention could be something like, *I intend to feel my ideal self as if I've already become it,* or *I intend to feel greater self-love,* or *I intend to see and feel my success.* Your intention is anything you want it to be.

Next, open your eyes and glance at the Ideal Self worksheet you created. Review your list for the first column, "Body". Then, close your eyes and see yourself already experiencing those things. For example, if you want to get six- pack abs, see yourself on the beach with your six-pack abs or see yourself doing sit-ups. If you want to heal chronic fatigue syndrome, see yourself feeling strong, laughing, and doing whatever you want to do without hindrance of any kind. The key is to really feel it as if it's already happened. This wires it into your brain, which we will talk more about later in the chapter. Go through your list and feel everything. Practice feeling the elevated emotion associated with it. For example, if you have acne, see yourself with clear skin, feel confident and beautiful, and feel yourself anew. In your mind's eye, look in the mirror and see your clear skin and smiling face shining back at you. This feeling produces chemicals that signal hormonal reactions in the body that will resolve your acne. It's brilliant. It won't happen by just doing it once or twice; you may need to do it consistently for several weeks or months, but it will happen, and it's not that hard. It's actually quite fun and satisfying, especially as you experience the results of your efforts.

When you are done *seeing* and *feeling* page one, move on to page two, and go through everything you wrote on all five pages, *seeing* and *feeling* each line as if it was already happening. Give yourself some time to do this, maybe thirty minutes at first. As you practice this, you will get quicker at feeling the end result feelings. Feeling those elevated emotions with the clear picture or intention you have in your head is a secret sauce to create the life you want. BUT you have to be willing to get still and practice this. Even when your Snapchat and TikTok are screaming at you, when you'd rather just chill with Netflix, or when it's more comfortable or familiar to sulk. Meditation means to get familiar with. So you will be building neural pathways in your mind for the way you want to experience life. As you do this, you become more and more familiar with these elevated feelings of support, prosperity, love, gratitude, excitement, and the like.

> Meditation means to get familiar with. So you will be building neural pathways in your mind for the way you want to experience life. As you do this, you become more and more familiar with these elevated feelings of support, prosperity, love, gratitude, excitement, and the like.

Spend as much time milking these good feelings as you can. It may be challenging at first, but stick with it. When your mind wants to get up, command yourself back to your breath and vision. Set a timer, and don't get up until you have felt the elevated emotions for an extended period of time. Twenty to thirty minutes is awesome, but five minutes creates neural pathways too. The practice is in returning to the focus when your mind wanders. This is where you are literally building your brain to reflect what you want to happen in your life. When you feel you have constructed the neural framework, you may open your eyes and go about your day. The key is to take your newly created energy into your day. Respond to life as your ideal self. This changes everything.

This is where you are literally building your brain to reflect what you want to happen in your life.

Your Morning Routine

A morning routine that orients you to your Ideal Self every day is key. Steven Covey said it best with his famous quote: "To know and not to do is not to know."

Your morning routine can be five minutes of complete focus, fully feeling each area of your Ideal Self for a full minute. You can commit to that, right? If you have longer, spend longer, but even just five minutes changes your neural pathways, teaches your subconscious who you are choosing to be, and activates your reticular activating system to notice opportunities that align with your Ideal Self. I teach you all about your reticular activating system later in this chapter. Committing to your morning routine of consciously creating your Ideal Self is the single biggest advantage you can give yourself, and it will serve you tremendously.

~~~

A study done on Olympians showed that when they reviewed their sport in their mind, the brain and muscles fired the exact same way they would when performing the actual activity. Another study took people who wanted to
~~~

learn to play the piano and split them into three groups: one group practiced, one group did not practice at all, and the third group only practiced in their mind. The group that only practiced in their mind did almost as well as the group that practiced on a piano. Practicing in the mind builds the neural pathways almost as well as practicing on a piano, and that is extraordinary! That's how awesome you are. Who's going to be doing sit-ups or backflips in their mind? Me!

I have always danced in my life. Remembering choreography happens on and off the dance floor. When I had dance competitions as a child, I would do the routine over and over in my head when I wasn't at rehearsal. Before a competition or audition, I would be almost constantly running the choreography in my mind to be sure I wouldn't forget the sequence of moves. Practicing it in my mind was the same as practicing it in full form. It created muscle memory just the same.

Dr. Joe Dispenza, the foremost neuroscientist researching and teaching this groundbreaking information, conducted a study where his team measured the immune response of participants. They measured a chemical in the blood called immunoglobulin, which acts as a major player in our immune response. His studies found that students who meditated once a day for four days had a 50 percent increase in immunoglobulin. Extraordinary! That's why my ninety-one- year-old grandmother is still going strong. She doesn't even know she's meditating, but she sits and watches the lake she lives on every day in gratitude for its beauty and her ability to enjoy it. I wouldn't say she has the best diet or is in shape, but she is very healthy anyway and incredibly strong. She takes time to be still, with love and appreciation. We can now see with science how that contributes to her long, strong life. The act of meditation itself is how you prevent a host of health issues that could potentially plague your future. But you will know better after reading this book how to prevent that. You will know that your thoughts and emotions create health in your body, so you can expect a long, strong, amazing life.

Growing up in the frozen tundra, just kidding, Illinois… it might as well have been the frozen tundra because, as a kid, I hated the winter weather. It seemed to last half the year. My birthday is April 16, and it snowed many times on my birthday. I remember it snowing a few times in May! The dis-may! My body and mind were most definitely ready for spring, yet gray coldness enveloped my environment. I made a firm decision to "live on vacation." We had taken a few family trips to Florida. Laying out on the beach in November was heaven to me. Have you ever experienced the disappointing feeling of the last day of vacation? I remember having the clear, powerful thought: *I will live on vacation; why wouldn't I?* As a kid, I knew nothing of the power of my mind and emotions in the way you are learning in this book. However, one doesn't need to be aware of the "secret sauce" for it to work for them.

The day after I graduated from high school, I moved to Hawaii. I had a boyfriend who was a couple of years older whom I had met on a summer job the previous summer. He went to college in Hawaii and invited me out. I was like, "Great!" We had an amazing summer, and I was welcome to stay and create my life there. However, I had a full-ride scholarship to a prestigious private college in Chicago and no scholarship or money to pay for college in Hawaii. And in those days, you went to college. Things are different now; there are so many entrepreneurial opportunities for you that didn't exist when I was college-age. There was barely the internet then... YIKES, right? I think the internet existed then, but it wasn't in every home and pocket. Watch a Seinfeld episode for a taste of what life was like before the internet and cell phones. It will blow your mind. You'll be like, "Why do they have to call their friend on their work phone lines? How is all this chaos happening because someone didn't get a message?" I caught an episode recently, and I was honestly stunned at how inconvenient life used to be.

Anyway, back to Hawaii. So I put my big girl pants on and came back to Chicago to attend college. I loved the school and my roommates and the amazing food in the cafeteria that was all free. It was like being on a cruise. But I HATED the cold weather. My body shuts down in that cold, dark weather. Well, not really, but that's how it felt. I didn't want to go to class, and it was painful to go outside, which was necessary to get anywhere, including the amazing cafeteria. I happened to start dating a guy that was from Tempe, Arizona. He invited me home with him for summer break. It took about one second to fall in love with the warm air in Arizona. I loved that everyone kept their doors wide open, with no screen doors and no bugs flying around. In Illinois, I didn't enjoy summer evenings outside because the mosquitoes are relentless, and they love my sweet blood. In Arizona, there are no mosquitoes! I just loved sitting outside and looking at the sky. I loved the monsoon season in August when the sky turns this cartoonish orange color, the wind blows, and hopefully, the refreshment of rain falls. I decided to stay in Arizona and leave my scholarship. I got a job as a cocktail waitress at a college bar near Arizona State

University and made plenty of money for a beautiful apartment and a beautiful life. I attended ASU on a resident's tuition. Palm trees lined my driveway; I was living on vacation.

After a few years in Arizona, I decided to move to Los Angeles, where I still reside. Palm trees and warm weather are still my daily experience. I am now working on creating the next level of *living on vacation,* which now, to me, means ocean views from every room.

My life follows my dominant intention and my vision. It doesn't always go as I expect, but according to Dr. Joe Dispenza, the manifestation always comes from the unknown, so if we are doing it right, it will never come how we expect.

How Does Imagineering Work?

We've talked about how this work will improve your physical health and keep you healthy and strong your entire long life. To recap, the biochemistry that is produced in your body when you are feeling elevated emotions of love, gratitude, joy, excitement, expectancy, and the like literally produces healthy cells. We've talked about how repeatedly cultivating these elevated emotions will wire them into your brain, making them much more accessible to you in waking life. If you struggle with depression, anxiety, or lack of motivation, your deliberate and consistent command to feel gratitude will make gratitude a dominant wiring. There are always things you can find to be grateful for. For instance, currently, two billion people on the planet do not have access to enough water for drinking and sanitation. Yeah. Think about that. Even the most "unfortunate" among us probably have at least two faucets where water, in any temperature desired, flows with a flick of the wrist. Modern life allows us to take for granted the basics, like having enough water. But if you allow yourself to really feel gratitude for that, you can walk around your day feeling blessed, and that is a good feeling. That is the feeling of winning.

> The biochemistry that is produced in your body when you are feeling elevated emotions of love, gratitude, joy, excitement, expectancy, and the like literally produces healthy cells.

This brings us to the questions that I know are burning inside your mind. How does Imagineering change anything in the outside world? How does it change my environment and change my opportunities?

This part is super fascinating. The neural pathways you build with your conscious intention then inform your world. Let me explain. Have you heard it said that life is like a hologram? Or that your brain is like a projector? Both are true. Your brain projects energy or frequencies out into the field around you, creating your life as a vibrational match to the energy or frequency you are emanating through your focus. Just like the 3D print analogy. We are printing out life based on the vibration, energy, and frequency that we emanate. We are living a vibrational match to our dominant energy. The key to this is that we can choose our dominant energy, vibration, and frequency. The hard part is choosing a higher frequency first and keeping it before the environment changes to match it.

> We are living a vibrational match to our dominant energy. The key to this is that we can choose our dominant energy, vibration, and frequency.

We all tend to "feel" according to our environment. We allow our environment to make us mad, sad, or irritated. By environment, I mean the people in your environment, the circumstances around your environment, and the physical space of your environment. We allow ourselves to be moved by outside circumstances instead of by inside choices. For example, say your parents are not ideal (I feel ya), and they create an intense environment at home sometimes. You can let the environment create your response of feeling shut down or like a victim, or you can choose not to let the environment dictate your energy and choose to feel empowered regardless of what's happening. You can also channel your choice into action by offering to help them with something that is irritating them instead of making yourself scarce when they are around. You will become adept at commanding your own positive, healthy energy, even when there are stressors in your midst. That is a superpower, a very useful superpower. You cultivate it with practice.

Let's make this really real. Say you have someone abusive in your environment. You overcome that in a couple of ways. First, you accept that the abusive person doesn't have much self-love, and their abusiveness is a reflection of their pain and suffering. It is likely they were abused in early childhood. In early childhood, we have mirror neurons absorbing everything in our environment, so it's likely that the root of their abusive programming is their own early childhood trauma. This doesn't excuse their behavior, of course. As adults, they are responsible for healing their childhood wounds, but unfortunately, not everyone knows to do that. If it's another child in the home being abusive toward you, please tell a loving adult in your life and get help. Second, you practice unconditional self-love and unconditional forgiveness (we get to Unconditional Forgiveness in Chapter 3). As you wire unconditional self-love into your brain, you will prune away any thoughts of victimhood. You will know that there is a purpose for good in everything, and you are stronger for everything that presents itself in your life. You will also be powerfully creating the end of any abusive experience through your unconditional self-love and practicing the Ideal Self Meditation. This brings me to the third thing to do: keep practicing the Ideal Self work; this is your main Imagineering exercise. This work will launch you out of any unwanted environment if you are consistent with it.

Staying in a creative orientation instead of a problem-solving orientation is key to creating life in alignment with what you want to create. Let me explain. A metaphysical tenant is that we are always creating what we are conscious of being. What are you conscious of being? Because how our thoughts are structured creates how we experience life, it's important that our thoughts are structured in a creative orientation instead of a problem-solving orientation. Inherent in the problem-solving orientation is the problem. If one is focused on a problem, then a problem will persist because we are always creating what we are focused on. For example, if you want to make more friends at school, focusing on not having enough friends won't bring you more friends. It will make you feel sad or shut down. Instead, your conscious focus is on having lots of new friends. Creating new friendships. See the difference? The difference is in how your conscious and subconscious mind interacts with what you want. You can see how when you have a consciousness for creating new friendships, you will have an open energy that will make you attractive to people. Here's another easy visual example: Let's say you want to get super fit. A consciousness of *I want to lose weight* has the problem inherent in the consciousness; instead, think, *I'm creating a super fit body*. We want to focus only on the end result, not what we want to change. Your world is a mirror of your consciousness.

> We are always creating what we are conscious of being.

> Your world is a mirror of your consciousness.

I love what the late great Anthony Norvell (1908-1990) says in his amazing book *Metaphysics: New Dimensions of The Mind.* He says when you awaken in the morning, there are two emotions that you should activate right away: the emotions of enthusiasm and expectation. He reminds us to use our emotions as energy boosters throughout our day. We can always choose to feel an emotion on purpose. Practicing this keeps you on your highest path. We must think and feel greater than our present circumstances if we wish to overcome them. I know some of us aren't comfortable having expectations for our day to feel wonderful. For some of us, we've been disappointed in people and life so many times that we are afraid to have higher expectations. We are afraid to expect great things. Isn't it interesting how we play these little games inside our minds?

> Use our emotions as energy boosters throughout our day. We can always choose to feel an emotion on purpose.

> We must think and feel greater than our present circumstances if we wish to overcome them.

For some of us, enthusiasm for life has been modeled for us by family and society. And for others, enthusiasm for life has not been modeled. Life can be hard when we don't know how it works. I get it. However, things will be different for you. You now have the practices that will allow you to consciously create your future in the Now moment. The key for you is to use these practices daily.

You will want to create a morning and evening routine. This is what will create your success. Just like going to the gym once won't give you results, it's the consistency that creates lasting change. Spend ten to twenty minutes at least, more if you want, in the Imagineering exercise taught earlier in this chapter. If you only have time to work on one area, then do that one area well. Train your focus on the end result feeling in that one area of your life or in as many areas as you have time for. I encourage you to make time to do all five areas every day. You can deeply feel the end result success in all five areas in five minutes once you practice and become adept at connecting with those elevated emotions. Spend more than five minutes when you can because spending more time creates faster change. Just like at the gym. Doing this every day will create amazing things in your life. You will show yourself the merit of this work.

A word of caution: Say you are visualizing and feeling that you got a part in a movie or that you are experiencing something desired, and then you don't get the part, or you don't get the girl, or whatever it is. Trust that everything is always working together for your good. Trust that you may not see the whole picture now, but there is something better on the horizon for you. The Bible says, "All things work for good for those who serve the Lord." The "Lord" means the great law of Life. God is the divine energy working through and as all things. The closer you live to God, the more Godlike you become. This isn't a religious sentiment, as God is not religion. Religions are merely the attempt at explaining God and creating fellowship and community. Frankly, any religion that thinks they are better than others or declares any gender identity or sexual orientation "wrong" has completely missed the point of God. God is love. God is inclusive. God has no judgment, no condemnation. God is in everyone, and God is for everyone. As someone who got a Ph.D. in Divinity, I can tell you all religions have the same core truths, dressed differently. There is so much I don't know, but I do know this: You are made in the image and likeness of the creator of the Universe. That means you can create. What can you create? Whatever is in your heart to create. I also know that you were perfectly made. You are God expressing itself as you. How could that not be perfect? Humans are designed to make mistakes and grow from them. Life is designed to give us feedback about who we are being in consciousness. We are human BEings, after all.

> You were perfectly made. You are God expressing itself as you. How could that not be perfect?

Do you know what the word "hu" means in human? It means God. It also means light. So you are a God Man BE-ing or a Light Man BE-ing. Light is vibration. It's an offering. You are a being who is offering your vibration to the world and magnetically attracting back that which is a vibrational match to your offering. This is why the better it gets, the better it gets, and the worse it gets, the worse it gets. This is why, in religion, we are taught to praise God in all things. Praise goodness, praise love, praise the almighty source energy. In praising God, the goodness of life, we are offering gratitude. We are declaring our wins before we see them. We are praising the good in the world, even when we feel stress. We are praising God for abundance, even if lack seems like a current reality. This praise is us putting our focus on what we want to see and feel. In all things, praise God means no matter what is happening in your life at the time, feel gratitude for your end results; your end results being the things you want to create. For example, getting into the school you want to go to or getting into the dance company. Perhaps your end result is being healthy after a diagnosis, or your end result is buying a car. Feel gratitude for the end result *before* you are in completion of it. This is praising God. Oh, and "man" in human means manifestation. We are God manifested. We are made to manifest. It's in the name of our species. All of us are manifesting everything we have; we just haven't learned how to use our manifestation power on purpose until now.

In his groundbreaking book *Becoming Supernatural,* Dr. Joe Dispenza tells the story of many of his seminar attendees who have mastered the art of teaching their bodies emotionally what their future feels like before the actual experience. He shares how his students learn to recondition their bodies and actually create new gene expression by embracing the elevated emotions of joy, gratitude, love, and inspiration. This is extremely significant information to have.

> We are made to manifest. It's in the name of our species.

Thoughts and feelings create your body and your life.

Are you familiar with *The Hidden Messages in Water* project by Masaru Emoto? I bring this up in this chapter because understanding this experiment and how it relates to your body and life is transformative. A Japanese scientist by the name of Masaru Emoto conducted many experiments to determine the effect our thoughts have on water. In his lab, he cryogenically froze water molecules and imbedded thoughts into them. He would project thoughts like *I love you* and *Thank you* into the water and photograph how the water molecule was affected by these thought forms. He would also use negative thoughts like *I hate you* and *You disgust me*. What he found can only be described as amazing. The water molecules that were told "I love you" had beautifully symmetrical crystals like a snowflake. The water molecules that were told negative statements were morphed, ugly, and even discolored. This study was conducted many times, and the same results were always found. Even when the words were written and taped to the petri dish, the effect was the same. Isn't that so interesting that the written word also has a vibrational offering? You can search *The Hidden Messages in Water* to see the photographs. They are truly astounding. The beauty of the water crystals, when told loving, positive things, cannot be overlooked. Think of how significant this is when you remember that you are about 90 percent water. What are the thoughts in your head? How are they affecting the waters of your body?

Masaru Emoto wrote many best-selling books to share his findings: *The Miracle of Water, The Secret Life of Water, The Healing Power of Water, Love Thyself: The Message from Water III,* and *The True Power of Water.* Reading these books is pure joy for me because isn't it fun to learn that water is magical? Water holds a key to our own magic. Most people take water for granted. I always find it funny that restaurants give water for free and dump it out when it's not used, yet water is the most valuable thing on the planet. We call water "the magical elixir of life" in my house. Having a greater understanding of the brilliance of the everyday things in life makes us naturally happier.

> We call water "the magical elixir of life" in my house. Having a greater understanding of the brilliance of the everyday things in life makes us naturally happier.

Use this information, and bless your water and your food before you consume it. Think about this in relation to the mirror exercises given in Chapter 1. Tell yourself, "I love you. I'm beautiful. I'm amazing just for being human. I am smart. I am talented. I am strong. I am wise. I am noble. I am creative. I am a genius." Know that by feeling this within yourself, you are creating greater physical health and beauty and creating circumstances that match your energy in your world.

It wouldn't be a chapter on Imagineering if we didn't talk about your spectacular reticular activating system. Get ready to dive into the depths of your brain and uncover one of its coolest superpowers. Buckle up because we're about to take a thrilling ride into the world of the reticular activating system (RAS) and how it completely skews your perception of life to what you are familiar with. Remember when I said that meditation means to "become familiar with"?

The RAS is your brain's bouncer. Imagine your brain is like a bustling nightclub, and the RAS is the bouncer at the door. This brain bouncer has a dual role—it lets in the VIPs (Very Important Perceptions) and keeps the non-VIPs out. In more sciencey terms, the RAS is a bundle of nerve cells in your brainstem that filters out unnecessary information, allowing you to focus on what really matters. There are literally billions of bits of information in our environments for us to experience. We can't experience all of it, so our brain filters it for us based on what we choose to focus on.

Think about the last time you were shopping for a new phone or pair of sneakers. Suddenly, it seemed like the whole world was flashing those exact items in your face! Was it a coincidence? Nope, that's your RAS in action. It's like your brain is shouting, "Hey, this is on your radar now, so let's notice it everywhere!"

Your RAS is also like your brain's personal assistant, always looking out for what you care about. Ever woken up thinking about a cool new hobby or dream vacation? Bam! Your RAS gets to work. Suddenly, you start seeing ads for that hobby class or vacation spot everywhere. It's not magic; it's your RAS serving up options you've opened your mind to.

The Spotlight Effect

Alright, let's get psychological for a moment. Ever felt like everyone is staring at that pimple on your nose? Or that your awkward dance moves are being broadcast on national TV? Well, surprise—that's the "spotlight effect" brought to you by your trusty RAS. Your RAS cranks up the spotlight on whatever you focus on. If you're focused on your insecurities, it's like you're broadcasting them in neon lights. But if you're rocking that self-confidence, your RAS is there, cheering you on.

From Goals to Reality

Guess what? Your RAS is also a GPS for your dreams. Imagine you set a goal—let's say, acing your math test. Your RAS locks in on that goal, and suddenly, you're spotting math study sessions, helpful YouTube videos, and even math memes (because why not?) all around you.

Ever heard the phrase "you attract what you think about most"? That's your RAS proving it's not just about luck; it's about your mindset shaping your reality. So, if you keep thinking about how amazing your day is going to be, your RAS will make sure it's packed with awesomeness.

Hacking Your RAS for Positivity

Time to drop some wisdom—you can totally hack your RAS to make your life brighter. It just feels good to feel good, so why would we want it any other way? Ready to turn up the positivity dial? Here's a game plan:

1. ***Set Clear Intentions:*** Whether it's getting good grades, making new friends, or becoming a ninja at playing the guitar, set clear intentions. Your RAS is like a search engine—the more precise the query, the better the results.

2. ***Picture It Like a Movie:*** Imagine your goal vividly, like a movie scene playing in your head. Feel the excitement, hear the sounds, and taste success. Your RAS doesn't know the difference between imagination and reality, so it treats your visions as real missions. Think about that for a moment. You are teaching your subconscious mind that what you are visioning has already happened; therefore, it's safe. Thus, your natural trepidation toward doing new and unfamiliar things will be dissolved because you have made it familiar with this exercise and the other exercises in the book.

3. ***Surround Yourself:*** Hang out with positive peeps who uplift your vibe. Your RAS takes cues from your surroundings, so make sure they're radiating good vibes. Chapter 4 is dedicated to this very subject. Who you allow to influence you is very important, as well as the influence you have on others.

4. ***Gratitude Attitude:*** Ever tried starting your day with a gratitude list? Your RAS loves this stuff. When you

focus on what you're thankful for, your RAS notices even more things to be grateful about.

> Think about that for a moment. You are teaching your subconscious mind that what you are visioning has already happened; therefore, it's safe.

This is a foundational exercise for me. I love writing, so it's enjoyable for me to wake up and put pen to paper in gratitude for the wonderful day ahead of me. This projects into my reality the vibrational match to my focused attention. Just as the pilot of a plane must set the course before take-off, you must set the course of your day before take-off. Spend a couple of minutes in gratitude, thinking about all that can go well that day. Focus on it all going just as you'd like. You will take the time to see and feel this into being-ness. Without taking the time to do this, you will just be creating, by default, from everyone else's focus around you. Your day will not always go as you vision; some days might go very awry, but continue to set your course each morning. Not setting your intention never did anyone any good.

> This projects into my reality the vibrational match to my focused attention.

The Reality Remix

Now, picture this, just for fun: Your brain is like a DJ spinning the tracks of reality, and the RAS is the mixer, selecting which beats to drop. You have the power to curate your own reality playlist—the songs of success, friendship, happiness, and all the good stuff. But it takes discipline of thought. The discipline of thought is not something we are commonly taught. We must all learn to choose our thoughts and feelings. This isn't always easy when stressful situations present themselves. Remember in these times that everything is for you. Ask yourself, *What is the gift or lesson in this stressful situation?* Sometimes, the gift or lesson is simply that you have an opportunity to overcome something with grace. This makes you practice your self-mastery. *That* is a gift.

> We must all learn to choose our thoughts and feelings.

We want to always be practicing our self-mastery. This means we are always practicing choosing our level of thoughts and emotions. It means choosing our vibrational offering to the world. It matters what energy you give off. It matters for your own life experience, and it matters in terms of what you are contributing to the world.

When I drop my sweet kids off at school in the morning, I always have a big smile on my face, greeting other parents, kids, and educators with joy. My smile generates other smiles. It's hard not to smile at someone when they are smiling at you, right? What a difference this makes for the entire environment when everyone is smiling. Isn't it true that when you walk into a classroom, and your teacher is smiling and happy to be there, it makes your time in that class better? We all know this, but I observe many adults who don't understand the power of their own energy and focus.

So, Dear Teenagers, train your reticular activating system to focus on what you want to see. In time, you will see, feel, and be more of that.

> Train your reticular activating system to focus on what you want to see. In time, you will see, feel, and be more of that.

I welcome you to send me an email with your feedback from doing these exercises to Blythe@BlytheNaturalLiving.com. I love hearing from you about how these practices have transformed your life and continue to bring greater possibilities for you. I read every email with the subject: **My results so far**. Keep up the great work, and keep me posted!

Chapter 3
3rd Key
Unconditional Forgiveness

You have had to forgive many people already in your life, I'm sure. For little things. Your siblings for taking your stuff and breaking it, your friend for ditching you that day, your teacher for saying something insensitive, or your parents for not understanding. You're already practiced at forgiving. You already express this superpower, although you may not realize it's a superpower.

When I was a teenager, visiting my grandmother at her home, she slapped me across the face for spilling water on her new carpet. Water. I don't know why I emphasize that it was water because I don't think I could name anything that warrants a slap in the face when spilled accidentally. But as a teenager, did I decide to resent my grandmother for that abusive, from my perspective, demonstration? Absolutely not, because we have the ability to let things go. I knew she wasn't a terrible person, she just had very outdated communication tactics.

Don't you wish all the grown-ups around you could let things go as easily as you? Some do, thank goodness, because don't we feel a difference between people who forgive easily and those who hold a grudge? Don't these two dynamics feel very different to us? Which one feels better in your body?

How it feels in your body is significant for many reasons. First, our bodies speak to us; this is intuitive communication. Most adults have never been taught that how their body feels is a communication from Source Energy. We get intuitive knowing through our bodies. You've experienced this when your gut suddenly feels unsettled or you get a tightness in your chest. Everyone's body speaks to them in a unique way, and it's up to you to decipher the message. However, usually, your mind knows exactly what your body is saying once you understand this as communication. When we are honest with ourselves, we usually know.

You know when you walk into a room, the energy dynamic in the room. You can feel when someone isn't telling you something. You know if you feel like you should not spend time with someone. You know if someone brings you down. You know the feeling inside you when you spend time with someone whose values don't align with yours. This is a quantifiable feeling in the body. This is something to pay attention to because the feeling is a guidance system, there to guide and direct you. To keep you on your highest path. Ask the happiest, most successful people in the world, and they will always tell you they listen to their gut, always. This is something that strengthens with practice. You will learn the subtle nuances of when you're feeling guidance from Life. This feeling is keeping you on the path to expressing that aspect of you that the world needs and that only YOU can express. It's just true that you are destined for greatness, and you get there with much more ease and flow when you develop the skills of following your intuition. More on intuition in my next book.

> It's just true that you are destined for greatness, and you get there with much more ease and flow when you develop the skills of following your intuition.

Back to forgiveness. So, you probably didn't know that by forgiving, you are a part of something so powerful in your life. Something that many institutions have spent millions of dollars studying. I include some of these studies in this chapter because I want you to know there is a big payoff for you when you integrate the wisdom of unconditional forgiveness into your life.

Forgiveness is a lifestyle; that's why I call it unconditional forgiveness. Everything is forgiven, not for the other person's benefit but for your own well- being. I know the art of this well. My father is someone who, frankly, always disappoints me. For example, I sent him a text to let him know this book was getting published, and he did not text back. My eight-year-old daughter and my husband have been producing a YouTube show since she was five years old called *Asta's Magical Life* (she named it). The videos are cute, educational, and well-produced. I would send my dad and stepmom the link to her videos, and neither would text back, ever. No response. So bizarre, right? I mean, I grew up with my dad in the house. I know you hear this, and it sounds like we're estranged or don't know each other, like he's a long-lost dad I never knew as a child or something. Nope, I grew up with him. What the heck? How can he not show any interest in his grandchildren or in the cool things I am doing in my life? I don't even think my dad knows I have a Ph.D.

This one time, I sent him a digital laser measuring tool for his birthday because he's a builder and always has a tape measure with him. I thought this was a really cool gift for him. He never even let me know he got it. When I called to ask if he had received it, he said, "Yes." Not even "thank you."

I constantly must forgive my dad. I just let things roll off me and not take it personally. I call him to see how he's doing, and the conversation consists of me asking him questions about his life, his dog, his boat, and his day, and he never asks me anything about what I'm up to or how his grandkids are. He never calls me, not even on my birthday most years.

The gift in this for me is that it gives me the opportunity to forgive. It has taught me that people don't need to be what I want them to be or expect them to be. I would love to have a completely different kind of father or a completely different kind of relationship with my father, but everybody gets to be who they are.

When we resent others or hold grudges, that's the same as saying, "You need to be who I think you need to be." That's not how to have a healthy, happy life. It's good to acknowledge that most people are just doing the best they can.

I remember being in the kitchen of my dad and stepmom's house when I was visiting for the holidays one year. My dad was sitting at the kitchen table, and his mother, my grandmother, was there. A conversation was sparked about how mean my great-grandmother was, my father's grandmother. It was revealed that she would lock my dad in the bathroom when she was babysitting him as a toddler. My dad shared this, so he remembered that. What a traumatizing experience for a toddler or young child to have. I would never treat my children with that kind of disrespect. I don't even agree with ignoring toddlers when they are having a tantrum. I never ignore my children, especially when big feelings are happening. In that generation, these kinds of tactics were commonplace, but it doesn't make it any less traumatizing for the child. If a child is abused for crying or being loud, it stands to reason that his communication faculties would shut down. That conversation let me see a side of my dad I had never seen—a wounded side.

Forgiveness Makes You Healthier

So we established that we know what it feels like to forgive and what it feels like to hold a grudge. We know what it feels like when others around us easily forgive and what it feels like when others hold a grudge. We want to stay in that feel- good place of easily forgiving others because it helps us maintain lifelong health. Tens of millions of dollars have been spent at various institutions studying the effects of forgiveness. It turns out that your body creates entirely different biochemistry when you are mad, resentful, bitter, annoyed, irritated, or just meh than it does when you are at peace, in joy, appreciation, gratitude, love, and the like. This is amazing news. The biochemistry that is created in the feel-good emotions regenerates your cells optimally.

See, your amazing thirty-eight trillion cells are always regenerating. You are always creating new cells. You can see this as your nails and hair growing or your skin healing after a cut, scrape, or burn. But your organs and blood are also regenerating constantly. Your body is truly a God technology, auto-renewing itself constantly.

However, when people live in the not-so-good feeling range of emotions, most often, the body remains in fight, flight, or freeze mode, thus creating a biochemistry that disallows optimal regeneration of cells. The body is pure genius, and everything is designed perfectly. When the body is in stress mode, it's not time to regenerate. The body uses its resources to prepare for fight, flight, or freeze. When people live in dis-ease, it creates diseases. Do you follow? We touched on this in Chapter 1.

So why am I telling you this in this book? Because this book is about giving you the exact keys to creating a life you love. Maintaining perfect physical and mental health is a big part of that. Too many people in their twenties and thirties are getting cancer these days, and it's because their bodies are acidic from living in dis-ease. Here are a few findings from various studies done on the power of forgiveness.

The Science of Forgiveness

Numerous studies have suggested a positive correlation between forgiveness and improved physical and mental health. Improved mental health seems obvious. We clearly will feel happier when we are not holding grudges. More on that in the coming pages. But I think it's particularly interesting that a lifestyle of forgiveness will make you physically healthier. Researchers have identified several ways in which forgiveness can contribute to better health outcomes:

1. ***Reduced Stress:*** Holding onto anger, resentment, or grudges can lead to chronic stress. Forgiveness involves letting go of these negative emotions, which can result in reduced stress levels. Lower stress is associated with better cardiovascular health, improved immune function, and a decreased risk of various stress-related illnesses.

2. ***Lower Blood Pressure:*** Studies have shown that practicing forgiveness can lead to a reduction in blood pressure. Chronic high blood pressure is a risk factor for heart disease and other cardiovascular issues, so this effect contributes to improved cardiovascular health. Tell your parents this one for sure! Heart disease is the largest cause of death in Americans. As a teen, I know it's not your concern now, but this information will ensure your lifelong health and vitality.

3. ***Enhanced Immune Function:*** The emotional burden of holding onto grudges and resentment can suppress the immune system's function. Forgiveness

can release this burden and allow the immune system to function more effectively, leading to improved resistance to illnesses.

4. ***Positive Emotions:*** Forgiveness is associated with positive emotions such as compassion, empathy, and gratitude. These emotions create the biochemistry that regenerates your cells optimally, maintaining physical health.

5. ***Decreased Hostility:*** Holding onto grudges can fuel feelings of hostility and aggression. These emotions create acidic biochemistry in the body, causing degenerative diseases in time if perpetuated. Forgiveness helps reduce these negative emotions, leading to more harmonious interactions with others and contributing to a healthier social environment.

It's important to note that forgiveness is a personal and often challenging process. It doesn't mean condoning harmful actions but rather choosing to release the emotional grip they have on your well-being. There's an old saying that I hope you're too young to know that says something like, "You can forgive, but never forget." That's wrong! True forgiveness is forgetting.

> True forgiveness is forgetting.

I have a friend who had a very intense thing happen to her. She dated a gorgeous, successful guy who literally drove her crazy. He cheated on her all over the place, and she knew it. Yet when she would ask him about it, he would deny it and call her crazy. Side note: No one can ever really lie to us. We always know when someone is lying to us. We feel the lie. Isn't it true? If we are honest with ourselves, we can feel when someone isn't being truthful. Learn what a lie feels like in your body. This knowledge will serve you very well. (I will share more intuitive tips in my next book.) She did know the truth; however, she let him convince her that it was all in her head, making her feel stupid and insecure. The ridiculous thing is that he knew the truth, and he knew she knew the truth, and he chose to contribute to delusion instead of the truth. He could have been honest and simply owned where he was at. Instead, on a rainy night in the desert, after overconsumption of alcohol and perhaps drugs of a white powdery nature, he nearly killed her in the front yard by repeatedly punching her in the face with all his might. And when I say almost killed her, that's not a dramatization. My friend would have died that night if she hadn't been rescued and taken to the ER by her father.

> No one can ever really lie to us. We always know when someone is lying to us.

As you can imagine, this was extremely traumatizing for her. Physical abuse was never present in him before. I know he was being investigated for felony theft with his businesses, and it was a high-stress time for him. He ended up going to jail for aggravated assault and pleading guilty to two counts of felony theft through his companies. Long story short, the relationship was obviously over, and it took time to heal from such an ordeal. There was mourning for what the good times were. She genuinely loved him before the incident but could never allow herself to be with him again.

As the next fifteen years unfolded, she would tell me stories about her dating experiences and when she would tell a new guy about what had happened. I remember telling her what I'm telling you, "You must forget." We must not keep the horrible things that have happened to us in our consciousness. It reinjures us and reinforces us as victims. Remember what you learned in the previous chapter: You are always creating what you are conscious of being. So being conscious of being a victim will create more circumstances for you to be a victim.

In my friend's case, how do you think those new guys who didn't know her well yet perceived her when she told them that story? Was she starting a potential new relationship in the Now, or was she bringing in the past? The worst parts of the past at that. We think we are wearing our pain as protection or something, but we really are just not living in the present. Forgiveness and forgetting put us in the Now, and the Now is the only place the magic can be.

> Forgiveness and forgetting put us in the Now, and the Now is the only place the magic can be

Everything in life happens for us, not to us. There is a lesson from every pain point you've ever had that will evolve you into greater versions of yourself. There's a point in our lives where we may graduate out of learning from pain or struggle and move into learning from joy, from connection, from success. This happens when we take the learning and allow ourselves to up-level. You are doing that by reading this book and practicing what it teaches you.

A quick word about the Now. We talked a little bit about the present moment, AKA the Now, in Chapter 2. When you're using the Imagineering techniques, you can only do it in the Now moment. The only place you can create from is the Now moment. However, many people create from the past by bringing the past into the Now moment. We are socialized to think that we are what we have already experienced. But we also are what we want to experience if we take the time to put our focus there. You can choose to bring with you throughout your life the learnings and the blessings that make you, You. But you don't need to bring with you the limitations you've experienced or that other people put on you. You don't need to bring with you the pain and victimhood. If you were the victim of something horrible, and I know that way too many kids have been, please know that it doesn't have to come into your Now moment or your future. Being in the Now means forgiving everything that has come before this Now moment if it's not serving your desired state. You really do have that power.

> The only place you can create from is the Now moment. However, many people create from the past by bringing the past into the Now moment.

The world loves you and needs you. Nothing can destroy the genius, the God technology that you are. Choose in the Now moment to know yourself the way God knows you, as a creator, capable of showing yourself your power, capable of creating a life you love.

> The world loves you and needs you. Nothing can destroy the genius, the God technology that you are.

You've likely heard the phrase, "The present is called the present because it's a gift." I love that. But also, the present is pre-sent. The present is pre-sent by your conscious awareness. You are pre-sending vibrational data for a life you love in every way when you do the exercises you learned in Chapters 1 and 2. This pre-sent vibrational data will become your present with consistency.

Remember the reticular activating system (RAS) in your brain that we talked about earlier? You Are Amazing, this is what I'm saying! Your brain filters what it's familiar with the way your social feeds filter what you've previously liked or shown interest in. Although your brain does a much more precise job. There are trillions of bits of information for your brain to process at any given moment, so it only makes you aware of the things that match your consciousness, leaving literally a world of possibility unnoticed by you all the time.

At a seminar I attended some time ago, a video was played with the instruction to count how many times the people moved their arms. I watched and counted as directed. After the video, the seminar instructor asked who saw the gorilla walk through the frame from right to left. I turned to my husband, who was sitting next to me, almost befuddled. A gorilla? What the heck is this woman talking about? There was no gorilla in that video. My husband said, "I saw it." I said, "What?" Then I realized why he saw it. He wasn't following the instructions to watch the arms. I'm sure he tuned out thirty minutes prior to those instructions, so his attention wasn't on counting the arm movements. Because his focus wasn't locked on a task in the video, he saw all of it or at least more of it; the giant gorilla that walked through the frame didn't escape his notice. This is the reticular activating system at work. It alerts us to the information we need, or that is familiar because there is way too much information available at any given moment. Much of that information isn't useful to us, and we simply don't need it. So your brain, in its wisdom, filters it. It filters it based on your subconscious and conscious minds. So, if you want more opportunities to find *you* in whatever areas in your life, become aware of information that is already there but going unseen. To do this, spend time doing the Imagineering exercises to teach your brain to filter information in support of what you want to create in your life.

If you experience challenging relationships with people, use your RAS to help you see the good in them. Your RAS is always taking instruction from what you're thinking about. For example, say you feel like your mother is critical of you, and you have this thought often. Your RAS will take instruction from that and will interpret criticism when perhaps she's not intending that at all. Or say your coach was hard on you once, and that stuck with you, your RAS will continue to interpret the coaching with that undertone. Instead, unconditional forgiveness helps keep that RAS slate clean from debris we don't want to see and experience. When we forgive easily, we set ourselves in the position of being able to receive different information. Moreover, when you deliberately choose to feel accepted, inspired, empowered, and free, you are giving your RAS the instruction to make you aware of circumstances that will make you feel accepted, inspired, empowered, and free. Get it? It's very cool. You, indeed, are amazing.

Forgiveness Makes You Happier

Without a doubt, those who easily forgive are happier. Like I stated above, it's very important that we understand the difference between forgiving and condoning. You always want to honor yourself and not allow others to mistreat you. Forgiving is not about letting someone abuse or mistreat you. Forgiveness doesn't mean that one should ignore or tolerate harmful behaviors, but rather, it's about finding a way to let go of the negative emotional burden for one's own well- being. You forgive for yourself, not for the other person. You forgive so you don't feel the burden of resentment or victimhood. You can forgive and still never engage with someone again if that is what feels best for you.

When we learn the art of unconditional forgiveness, our lives become naturally happier. If someone makes a comment you don't like, forgive it and don't think twice about it. It's raining on your birthday when you have a pool party planned; forgive it and dance in the rain. If you got a bad grade, forgive yourself and aim to do better next time. If your parents say no to something you really want, forgive them; they are likely looking out for your best interest or are just doing the best they can. Do you see how forgiveness is an ongoing way of life? It's cold outside, and you hate that, forgive it. Forgive whatever confronts you, and experience how this dissolves stress and anxiety before it starts.

Listed in the previous pages are some ways that science has shown how forgiveness makes you healthier. Below are some ways science has shown how forgiveness makes you happier.

1. ***Increased Positive Emotions:*** Engaging in forgiveness has been consistently associated with an increase in positive emotions such as happiness, joy, and contentment. Letting go of resentment and anger allows individuals to experience greater emotional well-being. This is obvious, yet I know many adults who don't live by this wisdom.

2. ***Improved Mental Health:*** Forgiveness is linked to lower levels of depression, anxiety, and other negative psychological states. By releasing the burden of holding onto grudges, individuals often experience improved mental health and a greater sense of happiness. Forgiveness offers a greater sense of control over one's emotions.

3. ***Enhanced Life Satisfaction:*** Forgiveness contributes to an overall sense of life satisfaction and well-being. When individuals can resolve conflicts and let go of negative feelings, they report higher levels of satisfaction with their lives. Again, this is obvious, I know, but unforgiveness is insidious, and many go unaware of the detriment.

4. **Reduced Rumination:** Dwelling on negative thoughts and replaying hurtful events can lead to rumination, which is associated with decreased happiness. Forgiveness interrupts this cycle by redirecting individuals' focus toward more positive and constructive thoughts.

5. ***Strengthened Relationships:*** Forgiveness leads to improved relationships, no doubt about it. Repairing damaged connections and fostering understanding

results in a happier social environment and a greater sense of belonging.

6. ***Enhanced Self-Esteem:*** Forgiving oneself for past mistakes or forgiving others for wrongdoings leads to improved self-esteem. This self-acceptance and self- compassion contribute to a more positive self-image and overall happiness. This then contributes to your ability to show up in the world as your full, authentic self. Being your authentic self is a gift to yourself and to the world. Always remember that.

7. ***Promotion of Gratitude:*** Practicing forgiveness can encourage individuals to focus on the positive aspects of their lives and the relationships they value. This shift toward gratitude is strongly linked to increased happiness for obvious reasons.

8. ***Reduced Stress:*** Letting go of grudges and resentment can alleviate stress, as these negative emotions often contribute to chronic stress. With reduced stress levels, individuals are likely to experience greater happiness and overall well- being.

9. ***Sense of Empowerment:*** Forgiveness involves taking control of one's emotions and choosing to let go of negativity. This sense of empowerment and agency can lead to increased happiness as individuals feel more in charge of their emotional well-being and ability to create their future as they choose.

10. ***Positive Coping Mechanism:*** Practicing forgiveness develops valuable coping skills that can be applied in various life situations. These skills contribute to better

emotional regulation and resilience, which are associated with higher levels of happiness.

11. ***Emotional Freedom:*** Holding onto grudges can trap individuals in a cycle of negative emotions. Forgiveness offers emotional liberation, allowing individuals to experience a greater sense of freedom, lightness, and happiness.

> Forgiveness offers a greater sense of control over one's emotions.

On the first date I went on with my husband almost twenty years ago, he took me to a crowded bar where we had to speak very closely to one another to hear each other. I remember saying, "Tell me something about yourself." To which he answered, "I have a son." We were in our early twenties in Los Angeles, and he had a five-year-old son in Estonia, where he is from. His heart was broken that he was away from his son, yet for whatever reason, in his own young and immature way, he couldn't be in Estonia for his own well-being. There was a lot that had transpired between him and his first wife. He got married at nineteen years old, had a baby at twenty years old, and was way out of his emotional league. For reasons I don't think he even understood, he left his country and left his son in the capable hands of his ex-wife and her new partner, who did an amazing job raising him. I met his son when he was nine years old in Estonia, and it was love at first sight for me. A beautiful relationship blossomed for us through Skype (the only video call at the time) when I returned to California. He visited Los Angeles, and we visited Estonia, and it seemed like we were a happy, unconventional family. Until one year when we visited with our then three-year-old daughter, who was the age he was when his father left him. Something was triggered in him during that visit, and he hasn't spoken to us since. That was five years ago, and his absence in our lives has left a hole in our hearts.

He hasn't expressed his anger or sadness or trauma to his father, my husband, for leaving. It's completely understandable that he would be hurt and mad. However, what he's telling himself isn't actually true.

If he's telling himself that his dad didn't love him enough to stay, that's not true. That's a story in his head. It's more accurate to say his father loved him very much and left him to be raised by the lovely man his mother chose, which broke my husband's heart at the time. My husband wouldn't make that choice as a man with more maturity, but as a twenty-two-year-old guy with a broken heart, that's what he did. It was traumatizing for both father and son, I'm sure. But doesn't the Now moment deserve to be fresh? Isn't it worth letting go of a story, especially a story that isn't true, for the sake of greater love now?

We had so many good times; I can't see how he wouldn't feel loved by us. But when unforgiveness is present, something will always be lost. Instead of living in the present, where he has two families that love him and two homes in different parts of the world to explore, he is choosing to be attached to past pain that has an untrue story attached to it. He's not yet ready to become conscious of his power.

Perhaps there's logic to thoughts like, *He left me, so I don't want to have anything to do with him*. But such thoughts don't serve his highest good and are just not true. These thoughts lack the nuances of the situation. Things are not black and white. If he could understand that leaving doesn't mean not wanting or not loving. You see how we make meaning out of things that really don't mean that. I want my stepson to forgive my husband for his own health and happiness. It makes me sad to think he's walking around his life feeling like a victim.

Life is always for you. Whatever has been hard for you has been for you. To help you establish compassion, awareness, or growth in some way. Whatever has felt like an obstacle is a stepping stone to take you to greater versions of yourself through growth.

> Life is always for you. Whatever has been hard for you has been for you. To help you establish compassion, awareness, or growth in some way. Whatever has felt like an obstacle is a stepping stone to take you to greater versions of yourself through growth.

My stepson is an amazing person who is very loved. If he feels abandoned, he must know that he's not abandoned at all in the present moment, and the present is all that really matters. We are with him energetically; we are for him. My daughter, who is eight years old at the time I'm writing this book, had a few fun holidays she remembers well with her older brother. She adores him and feels his absence from her life. In essence, we feel abandoned by him. I hope that doesn't sound insensitive; I don't want to downplay his experience. I don't know what he's feeling because he won't share his feelings with us or even speak to us. I pray he will forgive his father when he's ready. This will allow all of us to live in the present moment. I'm not sure he knows the heartbreak I feel about losing him because he's blocked all communication and lives on the other side of the world. He won't be able to hide forever, though; we are planning a trip to Estonia next summer. My husband insists we not ambush him if he doesn't respond to our outreach when we are there. But I disagree. I think when it comes to the people we truly love in life, we can't let un-truth prevail. Love always wins. What do you think? My email is at the back of the book; let me know.

I tell you this so you can see a story from a broader perspective. Most people are usually doing the best they can. When we realize this, we can let go of the ideals we have for people. Sometimes, people make mistakes, and we have the opportunity to grow by forgiving. Sometimes, we just must accept that someone's choices hurt us. Again, I never mean to condone anything abusive or illegal. Those types of behaviors should never be tolerated. I'm talking about the mistakes that people you love will make from time to time in life and the mistakes you yourself may make. Self-forgiveness is probably the most important aspect of unconditional forgiveness.

I want to say one quick thing about the word "mistake." I used that word in the above story, but it's worth mentioning that what we think are "mistakes" at the time can turn out to be the biggest blessings in our lives. Let us never really judge things in our lives as good or bad. That's the lifestyle of unconditional forgiveness. Unconditional forgiveness is really a stance that everything is for you. Whatever appears against you, when you can easily forgive it, becomes something that takes you higher.

> Whatever appears against you, when you can easily forgive it, becomes something that takes you higher.

You become an evolved presence in other people's lives when you have a habit of unconditional forgiveness. People will feel your relaxed nature. There's an energy of forgiving the traffic instead of cursing the traffic. Not in a silly formal way, but in an I easily forgive and release every irritation way. Feeding irritation or upset with your attention will make it bigger, leading you down the road to creating more things to be irritated and upset about, like we discussed in Chapter 2.

> Feeding irritation or upset with your attention will make it bigger, leading you down the road to creating more things to be irritated and upset about

There you have it, my Dear Teenager, the third key to unlocking an amazing life. Like all the keys, it's one to adopt as a lifestyle. You will be forever blessed by it.

Chapter 4
4th Key
Staying Influenced by Those You Admire

Staying influenced by those you admire may seem like an obvious concept, but its importance cannot be overstated, especially in today's world, where digital interactions and social media play a significant role in shaping our perceptions and emotions. As teenagers navigating the complex landscape of online interactions, it's crucial to recognize how often we allow ourselves to be affected by individuals who do not contribute positively to our well-being. This chapter delves into the power of conscious influence, self-awareness, and learning from those we admire to shape our personal growth and success. It also reminds you of the influence you have on others and to use that influence wisely.

The Impact of Unwanted Triggers

In a world dominated by social media, it's easy to find ourselves triggered by the opinions and behaviors of others, particularly those we don't admire or respect or even know personally. When someone triggers us, whether through a rude comment, a confrontational stance, or misinformation, it's important to pause and reflect on the impact this trigger is having on our emotional well-being. Recognizing that someone's negativity or hostility is influencing our mood and mindset can be a powerful wake-up call.

I have experienced this many times as a content creator who challenges prevailing norms around healthcare. In my Blythe Natural Living YouTube channel, I often discuss alternative approaches to health, like using herbs to reduce inflammation or exploring natural cures for cancer. I often receive comments from individuals who vehemently disagree with my views. These comments, while triggering if I'm not centered, serve as a reminder that not everyone's opinions are worth internalizing. In this case, the people leaving these comments are fighting for their limitations. In essence, they are saying, "No, there is nothing that can help me, my body is NOT designed to heal itself." Henry Ford was right when he said, "Whether you believe you can or you believe you can't, either way, you are right."

So, instead of letting someone's limited consciousness deter me, I have learned to discern between valid criticisms and baseless remarks, allowing me to stay true to my message of empowerment.

I've come to realize it's actually quite funny and interesting when someone thinks they know all there is to know. Someone might quote a bit of outdated science or declare something as fact that's not actually fact. Here's the truth: There is so much we don't know. We can only "know by scientific evidence" that for which we have instrumentation to measure. So, if we don't have the instrument to measure something, we don't "know" it. For instance, science doesn't provide us with evidence that we have a soul; there isn't an instrument to measure that. Therefore, any discussion of our soul or spiritual connection to the creator of the Universe goes unproven or is not "scientific," so for many, it's BS. This need for scientific evidence of everything distracts us from our own *knowing.* We are allowed to just know something because we know it. To feel something because we feel it.

> We are allowed to just know something because we know it. To feel something because we feel it.

When it comes to teaching others, we want to have data to back up certain things, but not everything requires data for real learning and growth. For instance, I have received the premiere intuitive training our world has to offer, or so I think. I don't know of any other intuitive training like the group I train with at Superconscious Intuition, through Conscious Education Company. While there is compelling data from intuitive studies, it's not these studies that I remember or learn from. I've learned by using the techniques and feeling it in my body. I learned the language and how intuitive information is communicated from the field to my body. I've learned by watching and experiencing incredible things happen. So when someone barks science at me as the prevailing end-all, I know they don't realize how much there is to know, how much science doesn't yet know, and how wonderful that is. It actually means we are living in a time-space reality that is far greater than commonly understood. There is so much more than logic and reason and three dimensions. Metaphysics gave me a taste of the truth, and it's delicious.

Embracing Your Unique Voice

As teenagers, it's essential to develop a strong sense of self distinct from external influences. Of course, this Self will continue to evolve. This chapter encourages you to embrace your uniqueness and authenticity. Even if your friends, family, or peers disagree with your beliefs or choices. Remember that your thoughts and feelings are valid. In fact, diversity of thought is what drives progress and innovation. Just because someone doesn't share your perspective doesn't mean your perspective is any less valuable.

As you navigate through life, you'll encounter people who challenge your views. Rather than succumbing to doubt or insecurity, use these encounters as opportunities for growth. Challenge yourself to question your beliefs, not to please others, but to reinforce your own convictions. This is a journey of self- discovery and empowerment, where you learn to stand firm in your principles without the need for constant validation.

Choosing Positive Influences

In the realm of social media, it's easy to be bombarded by a multitude of voices and opinions. To stay influenced by those you admire, it's crucial to filter out the noise and actively choose the sources of inspiration that align with your values and aspirations. Identify individuals whose messages resonate with you and whose accomplishments you admire. These could be thought leaders, authors, educators, photographers, filmmakers, artists, scientists, entrepreneurs, or whoever is making an impact in fields that interest you.

Follow their work closely, whether through their books, blogs, podcasts, or social media accounts. Engage with their content not only for entertainment but for the valuable lessons and insights they offer. Remember, staying influenced doesn't mean imitating others; it means drawing inspiration from their success stories and incorporating their wisdom into your own unique journey.

My life has been massively upgraded by several people whose work I study and follow, like Dr. Joe Dispenza, Neville Goddard, Psi Tek, and many more. But lately, there is one person who stands out above the rest as being so influential in how I set up my day for success, every day, and that's Chris Duncan, author of *You're Not Broken* and *The Superconscious Path* and the founder of Conscious Education Company. In CEC's flagship Magnetic Mind program, he teaches what they call "the Core 4." These Core 4 statements are so clear, simple, and brilliant. They set me up with a creative structure for my day. Even though I had a Ph.D. in Metaphysical Sciences before joining Chris Duncan's Magnetic Mind program and had many statements, affirmations, and declarations that I used, he taught me something so clear and powerful that it's what I use every single day to make sure I'm in the right structure for creating a life I love. The influence that he has had on my life through his programs is truly incredible. Isn't it profound how when one person follows their own genius and doesn't shy away from their own self-expression, that expression then goes forth to help and bless others? In his case, he was a businessman who owned gyms, hair salons, and a digital marketing school, but he knew he was meant to serve in a deeper way. His own journey led him to the understanding of his own Superconscious and how to create our reality by recoding our subconscious wounding and taking aligned actions toward our end results. Once he understood that, he was compelled to share it with others, and in so doing, ignited his passion, his genius, his sustained wealth, and a movement toward upgrading cultural consciousness. Big stuff happens when you trust and follow your own genius.

I feel you asking me, "What are the Core 4 statements?!" I have Chris's permission to share the Core 4 with you. They are:

1) I choose to live a life I love, and it feels like… (FEEL IT, what does it FEEL like? Refer to the Ideal Self exercise in Chapter 2.)

2) I choose to be healthy and vital, and it feels like…

3) I choose to be the predominant creator of my life, and it feels like…

4) I choose to live my true nature and purpose, and it feels like… (Your true nature is to be a creator,

and your purpose is found in your talents, gifts, and desires.)

The key to these statements, as we discussed in Chapter 2, is feeling the end result. It's the *feeling* that wires your brain and teaches your subconscious that you have it already. And it's the positive, elevated feelings that create healthy biochemistry in your body. These statements are powerful to do first thing in the morning and anytime to get in touch with your power and joy.

Learning From Other's Successes

Success leaves a trail of lessons and strategies for others to follow. While it's true that everyone's success journey will be unique, you can learn from other's successes and failures. If you aspire to excel in a particular area, whether it's photography, blogging, art, music, medicine, interior design, psychology, teaching, business, or whatever expression your genius takes, seek out individuals who have achieved success in those fields. Study their methods, observe their marketing strategies, and analyze how they have cultivated their unique brand. While imitation may be considered a form of flattery, the aim here is obviously not replication but education and inspiration. What's working for them? How can you take that information and use it to create success for yourself in any area of your life?

For instance, imagine you're passionate about photography. Look for photographers who are making a living with their art and see what they're doing. Maybe they are selling to stock libraries, or maybe they are using a drone camera to shoot properties for realtors and making good money at that. Maybe they are using a print-on-demand service you have never heard of and are putting their photographs on journals, T-shirts, and wall art. Watch how they market that. Watch what they do. While you shouldn't copy their marketing messages, you can certainly adapt their techniques to create something that is uniquely yours. This process of learning from successful people while infusing your personal essence is what ultimately helps you refine what you want to offer and establish your own identity as an artist, entrepreneur, lawyer, hairstylist, or whatever direction you want to take.

A personal, instead of professional, example of this could look like: Say you want a better relationship with your mom or dad, and you see that a few friends have really great relationships with their parents. You can ask them what they think are the top reasons for the connection they have with their parents. They might have to ponder it for a few moments; they perhaps have never thought about that before. After taking in the question, they respond back with a few insights that are very helpful to you. Perhaps one friend says that she and her mom have a date a few times a month, just a special time for the two of them that she really likes. If that is something you aren't presently doing with your mom, you realize that there is something fun you can create in your relationship that will bless you both, so you decide to enroll your mom in a monthly or twice- monthly fun time date. Or a friend tells you he runs with his dad when his dad gets home from work. You can tell from the way he tells you that he really enjoys this time with his dad and that it's healthy for them and their relationship. Maybe this inspires you to lead up family fitness at your house. I'm sure your parents will appreciate the leadership, and it will make them healthier and happier. Or say your parents aren't into any of those things, so you decide to meet them where they are. Ask them what brings them joy and happiness and do more of that together as a family if it's something you enjoy too. Do you see how we can allow others to influence us in ways that serve us greatly?

Embracing Lifelong Learning

As a teenager, you're at the cusp of a lifelong journey of learning, growth, and self-discovery. Your current interests and talents are just the tip of the iceberg, with countless opportunities waiting to be unearthed as you progress through life. Embrace this idea of continuous learning and expansion.

Your generation has a unique advantage—access to a wealth of information, online resources, and inspiring individuals. Seize this opportunity to not only develop your existing skills but also explore new ones. Allow yourself to be influenced by a diverse range of sources, from contemporary thought leaders to historical figures whose wisdom continues to resonate. Remember, the journey of self-discovery is ongoing, and your capacity to evolve and adapt is boundless.

Staying influenced by those you admire is a conscious choice that involves guarding your mental and emotional well-being, embracing your authenticity, and learning from the successes of others. As a teenager, the digital age presents you with both challenges and unprecedented opportunities. By cultivating a discerning mindset, nurturing your unique voice, and seeking inspiration from those who have paved the way, you can embark on a transformative journey of self-growth and personal empowerment. Embrace diversity of thought; we don't all have to agree. Adapt and innovate where new thought is needed, and remember that the path to success is not about replicating anything that's been done before but about infusing your own essence into every endeavor. Through conscious influence and self-awareness, you will navigate the complexities of the digital age with resilience, grace, and a deep sense of purpose.

We must always have a decerning mindset. Having a discerning mindset means that you know that everything that's published isn't the Truth. You know not every constructive criticism is valid, and not every opportunity is the right opportunity for you. You understand that the world is big and there is enough room for everyone to have their own life experiences. Something can be absolutely right for you and absolutely wrong for someone else. It always goes back to the feeling in your body; what does that Yes feel like? What does a No feel like, as a physical sensation in the body? This will help you tremendously as you navigate all the opportunities ahead for you. You will be faced with having to make decisions. This is one of those times when I don't think there are ever "mistakes." I think whatever choices you make will have their own lessons and growth. But when you start to check in with your higher self about what decision to make, you will find you are on a happier path with more flow and ease. It's just much more fun on that path.

> But when you start to check in with your higher self about what decision to make, you will find you are on a happier path with more flow and ease.

Don't Underestimate Your Influence on Others

Like really. Have you ever thought about how you influence others? How your moods and energies are impacting those around you? Take a look at how you make others feel. Sometimes, how others feel in relationship to us is more influenced by how they are feeling about themselves than our energetic imprint. However, observe the actual power you have to lighten the mood of the house when you bring more joy into the house. Observe how you can change your parents' willingness to give you more freedom when you show up with behavior that radiates responsibility and self-care. You are in the driver's seat a lot of the time with how your parents show up for you. Your parents will likely feel more comfortable giving you more freedoms when they see you showing up in a certain way. When you're helpful and attentive in the family and contribute your light to the family, you will see your parents respond favorably to that.

It's particularly important to realize the impact you have on your siblings, especially your younger siblings, if you have them. It's heartbreaking for me to witness some of my clients so traumatized by the bullying they received in their own families. Especially girls who are bullied by older brothers. When left unhandled by the parents who are supposed to protect them, it leaves a mess of fear, distrust, and low self-worth. Lots of terrible things happen as a result of older siblings introducing drugs, violent shows, movies, and sexual content to their younger siblings, who are in no way emotionally ready for this exposure.

Siblings have a beautiful opportunity to create a team-like mentality with each other that makes each other stronger. You want to have the "I got your back" attitude with your siblings. We should be each other's allies, not enemies.

If you're an older sibling to younger children, you have an amazing opportunity to nourish their lives. They are looking to you. Whatever you do, you are normalizing that for them. So if you vape and they see you vaping, you are normalizing that for them, making it more likely that they might want to vape. If you have a bad attitude toward your parents, you are modeling that for them. If you make a stink about eating your vegetables, you may influence their dislike of vegetables because they look up to you and think you're right about stuff. This is a position you didn't ask for, but alas, you have the honor of having, so I implore you to use your influence heartfully. You are in a position to make your siblings' lives better and vice versa. Support one another, cheer each other on, and protect each other from ridicule from those you associate with.

It's not just your siblings that you have tremendous influence over. You hold this position with your friends as well and with other kids at school and in your neighborhood. I can look back and see the influence certain friends had on me, some positive and some not-so-positive. I can see how being around friends who put an emphasis on style and fashion inspired me to do the same. I can see how being around friends who took their talents seriously and worked to cultivate those talents helped nourish my own. I can credit a boyfriend I had when I was eighteen for teaching me how to be a kind person. I know it sounds strange to say, but I didn't learn true kindness from my parents. They didn't model that. Even though they were church-going and productive members of society, I didn't learn deep kindness by watching them. I don't feel they were particularly kind to me. My mom would scream, yell, and hit to get us to church on time. There was stress and fear in my childhood. I feared my mother. She parented as a bully, one who yells and beats. An authoritarian whose rules were to be followed and never questioned. That doesn't make for a relaxed childhood. I would never treat my children the way I was treated as a child. That said, I didn't see this deep kindness in my world. When I dated this great guy, he opened a world of kindness that I had never experienced before. It was an unconditional kindness, not won from meeting expectations, but just offered of itself, for kindness's sake. I'm sure this had a huge impact on how I parent my children nearly two decades later. The impact we can have on each other is amazing. And if you're wondering, of course, I fully forgive my mother. She was a product of her environment. The past doesn't matter; I engage with her in the present, where she's quite fabulous now that she doesn't have four young children driving her crazy. She didn't have the tools you are learning in this book.

Be mindful of how you influence your friends and peers. Look for opportunities to be a positive charge in their lives. For instance, if you want to create more fitness in your life, you can start a running group with friends if school track and field isn't your thing or not in season. Or maybe you want to create a dance group. Head it up, choreograph something, and organize to meet at a park to rehearse. Maybe you start a book club with friends and bring back reading books! Maybe you start a Creation Group and use this book and the accompanying *I Am Amazing Workbook for Teens* as your course material to do together and share your wins in the meetings. It's powerful to hear each other's wins when manifesting new experiences in life based on the conscious direction of thoughts and feelings. It happens faster when you practice in a group because you create a morphogenic field, which is a fancy way of saying your individual vibrations join together and make everyone stronger. It's like if you each have a magnet, but you put all the magnets together, the magnetic pull will be so much stronger, therefore drawing life experiences that match it quicker. Reading this book in a group setting and doing the exercises together is a fantastic way to up- level your whole group of friends and/or family. Make big waves, baby! There are so many ways you can influence others positively, and in doing so, you always create a blessing for yourself.

Speaking of good influences, I'd like to take one more opportunity in this chapter to be a positive influence on you by reminding you of the importance of never sharing people's secrets unless, of course, they are in danger. When you tell someone something that someone told you in confidence, it tells the person you're telling that you can't be trusted. Someone I love very much, so I can't reveal their identity, does this all the time. She is always telling me about other people's business. So naturally, I would never share with her anything that I didn't want everyone in our circle to know. Makes sense, right? I can see plainly that she doesn't mind sharing other people's troubles or personal issues that have been conveyed to her. I usually change the subject or take a tangent away from other people's business. I know if there is something I need to suss out with someone close, it won't be her.

I was at a child's birthday party recently, and the child's grandmother quickly threw her daughter (the birthday girl's mother) under the bus. She doesn't know me or what I do and promptly shared very private information about her daughter. I was literally speechless. What words could I possibly conjure up to respond to a statement that was so clearly none of my business? The child's mother is someone who struggles with depression and anxiety quite a bit. I immediately got a glimpse of the dynamic between her and her mother and how that contributes to her sense of fear in the world. I mean... if you can't even trust your own mother not to tell everyone she meets about your greatest shadows, that's going to create a sense of fear in the subconscious mind.

If someone asks me if I can keep a secret, the answer is that I can keep a happy secret, but not a gossipy secret, so don't tell me. If you want to share with me some exciting news you can't tell anyone else yet, I'm your girl. I will celebrate with you and keep my lips sealed. But if you want to tell me gossip, I'm not interested. When we hear gossipy type news, it's too juicy not to share. It's like we have to share. "Did you hear..." I don't want to find myself talking about other people unless it's celebrating them. I know it seems like we are showing care and concern when we discuss loved one's affairs with others. But, if you want to show care and concern, speak to the person directly instead of speaking about them to others. You can always preface a hard conversation with "I love you, so I'm looking out for you, and I'm concerned about this..." When someone can see that your heart is in helping them, they are less likely to be defensive.

One of my favorite metaphysical tools is dynamic concentration. One great way to use dynamic concentration is to rehearse conversations you need to have with people in your mind before having the conversation. It's very important when you do this to create peace and stillness first. Sit down and close your eyes. Take several deep breaths to center you in your power of knowing. After a few breaths, when you feel relaxed and ready to focus, conjure up a scene where you are telling someone something you need to say. Make this scene real. What are you wearing, where are you, what's the environment, the temperature? Feel yourself meeting up with this person. Feel yourself feeling relaxed and confident as you share whatever information you want to share with them. Then, and this part is important, feel them receiving the information you've shared with an open heart. Feel them responding in the way you want them to respond. Feel yourself receiving that desired response. Feel the entire conversation as easy and kind. Now, feel yourself saying goodbye and the conversation ending. You can do that a few times if you need to, to prepare for difficult conversations. By doing this, you establish the blueprint for the conversation to go the way you want it to. By taking time to establish this blueprint in consciousness first, you affect how the other person responds to you. Crafting a response congruent with your desires.

This is also a great tool to use when you want to hear good news. You can follow the same method to conjure a scene where you hear the good news, the news you've been waiting for. You must hear this in your mind and respond in consciousness the way you would respond in waking life when you receive such great news. You must feel that excitement, feel that burst of energy, feel that joy, feel that gratitude, feel that sense of creatorship in your life.

I've had this experience so many times in my life. Sometimes, it's subtle; you almost don't recognize the connection right away between what you visioned and what happened, and sometimes it's so strikingly exact to how you visioned it that there is more joy in feeling your creatorship than there is in manifesting whatever it is you wanted.

About ten years ago, I was spring cleaning my room and caught a glimpse of my bare mattress from the sides and bottom, and it was sad. Very sad. It had what can only be described as some kind of mold creeping on the sides. I can barely type those words without cringing. I mean, a moldy mattress! That can't be my life! I quickly threw it away before any research was done for a new mattress. Being the eco gal that I am, I knew I didn't want a mattress that had anything toxic in it. Turns out, mattresses are pretty darn toxic. So, an organic mattress it is! Well, the one I fell in love with was nine thousand dollars, and dare I say, I was pretty broke at the time. I remember looking at the Naturepedic website and feeling like I had to have one. I played a scene in my mind's eye where I asked the owner if I could create a marketing video for his brand in exchange for a mattress, and in my visioning, he happily said, "Yes." I was promptly invited to an event at the NaturePedic showroom in Beverly Hills. I don't remember the details of how that happened (miracle), but I found myself at a beautiful event with TV stars and media. I was introduced to the owner as a host of a healthy lifestyle show; I was in production on my Blythe Natural Living show at the time. He greeted me with a smile and asked me with sincerity if there was anything he could do for me. I said, "Well yes, I'd love to create a marketing video for you, tell your brand's amazing story, and in exchange, I'd love a mattress." He happily said, "Sure," and introduced me to the showroom manager to arrange the details. I could almost feel in his energy like, *Why am I doing this?* We delivered a great video, and they gave me a beautiful mattress. When the manager was asking me which one I wanted, I told him the model and in a Queen size. He said, "Oh no, you need a King; you have to have a King and a topper too." They even threw in two amazing organic pillows and an organic mattress cover. Astounding, right? Little did I know I would get pregnant just a few months later, and we would need that King-size bed to co-sleep with our baby.

Another time, I was envisioning receiving funds to get my beauty accessory invention, MoisturEyes™, to market. In my visioning, an old friend came to mind. Someone who always wants to tell me how much money he has lying around—literally lying around or buried in coffee cans in the backyard. He doesn't believe in banks. (He's a Vietnam vet and doesn't trust the government, so instead of investing his surplus, he hides it. You can see how his lack of forgiveness and personal power have cost him millions because instead of earning interest for the last sixty years on his money, he hasn't. The opportunity cost of that is seven figures, no doubt.) So, because he came to my awareness, I gave him a call to check and see how he was doing. He asked me what I was up to, and I told him about my amazing invention. He promptly said, "Can I get in on that?" I said, "Sure!" He said, "How much do you need?" I said, "Twenty thousand for now." He said, "Sure, come get it."

Now, that technique has not always rendered me such wonderful results. Plenty of times, I haven't gotten what I thought I wanted at the time. Sometimes, I think there is divine protection in that. We have no way of knowing for sure. But it feels good to think that I'm spared from desires I had that might have jeopardized my sense of peace. I think when we are visioning and creating what is aligned with our highest good, that's when the magic happens. That's when we feel those moments of profound beauty and connection with life. That's when we see other people move in accordance with the blueprint we created in consciousness.

> That's when we see other people move in accordance with the blueprint we created in consciousness.

So, Dear Teenager, be aware of your influence on others. It is a superpower you have. Use it to up-level others and yourself. You will never go wrong by being kind.

> You will never go wrong by being kind.

Writing Exercise: Write down several ways you can influence others for the better. How might you have a positive influence on others?

Chapter 5
5th Key
Micro-Investing ~ Invest a Tiny Seed and Grow a Forest

Once upon a time, in a land not so far away, there lived a group of teenagers who discovered a magical secret. They realized that by planting tiny seeds of money and watching them grow, they could cultivate a forest of wealth. These brave young souls understood the power of micro-investing, the art of turning a few dollars into something grand. So, grab your shovels, my friends, and let's embark on a journey to uncover the joys of conscious wealth-building!

Man, I wish my parents or school taught me about money. I was in my twenties when I tried to start a business with absolutely no established credit. What's credit? I didn't have any. Don't get me started about my thirties. I cringe thinking about the money I blew without investing any of it. I lived well, I had expensive handbags, but I wasn't looking out for my forty-year-old self, who found herself painfully not at all where she wanted to be financially. So, I write this because after you read this chapter, you will know what I didn't know at your age or in early adulthood, and if you act on it, you will be on your way to creating wealth for your future self. Let me tell you, your future self will love that. And by future self, I don't mean retirement; I mean when you're young and want to start a business or buy a property or travel around the world. You will be able to do all of it if you know how to multiply your money with time.

The great news is that there are so many user-friendly micro-investing tools out there for you. Not to sound all old and stuff, but when I was a teenager, micro-investing tools that live in my pocket were not available to me. The concept of micro-investing wasn't born yet. Investing was something you did when you had thousands to invest, and it wasn't something that teenagers could get into on their own. But now, micro-investment tools are an app on your phone, and it's as easy as setting up an account and putting any sum of money into it. Even ten dollars a month, or whatever schedule you set up, or at any random time you want to deposit. This is an amazing advantage that generations past did not have.

Now, picture this: you're standing in front of a vending machine, contemplating your choice between a chocolate bar and a bag of chips. But what if instead of munching, you invest that money? Yes, that's right! Just a few dollars, planted in the right place, will sprout into a mighty tree of financial prosperity in time.

Forgoing the chips and soda to put those five dollars in your Acorns account is fun unless you're hungry! It's also fun to watch that number rise. What's an Acorns account, you ask? I will break down some excellent micro- investing tools at the end of this chapter. You can do your own research, too, to feel out which is best for you.

If you think you don't have money to invest, you're incorrect. Money goes through your hands. If you want more money to flow through your hands, start focusing on that with the Imagineering work you learned in Chapter 2. Ideas will come to you for ways to create money. What are you good at? What do you like to do? How can you bring value to others through these things? For instance, are you good at organizing and love color coding files, or do you find it very satisfying to organize a pantry or closet? If so, make some flyers or business cards and pass them around your neighborhood or to the parents in your school community. Many people need help with organization and are happy to pay for that. When you help someone in a way that's significant to them and fun for you, and you make money doing it, that's a recipe for success. It feels good to help people in a way that's easy for you, and it feels great to receive money. I'm sure every person reading this has something that they could offer their community and get paid for it. Maybe you teach a dance class for younger kids at the park and charge five dollars per kid per class or twenty dollars a month. You can post flyers around your park and neighborhood. Say ten people sign up; that's two hundred dollars per month for one dance class a week. That's four hours of work a month, besides the time spent making and posting the flyers. You can start a Stripe account for free to take payments and use a QR code right on the flyer to register and pay. Boom, you're in business.

The truly wonderful thing about that is that you will be giving a child a dance class that may not be able to dance in a regular studio. I don't know how much dance class costs elsewhere, but in Los Angeles, where I live, kids' dance costs at least 150 dollars a month, so perhaps not every child who wants to dance gets to be in a dance class. But taking a dance class out on the green at the park is just as great. There's music, there's choreography, and the child feels the movements and the music in their body. It's fun. Do you see how impactful that could be for someone? It's not just about you making money; you are giving something of so much value to others through what you are offering. Remember that.

> It's not just about you making money; you are giving something of so much value to others through what you are offering. Remember that.

If you want to make money outside the traditional job structure as a teenager, think about what you could offer that people will pay for. People will pay to have tutors for their younger kids. Could you tutor in math or reading or another subject? People will pay to have their yards and gardens tended to. This is awesome work in the sun if you like relating to plants. I love plants. (Sidebar: Spend more time with plants. Observe them, observe their geometry. Watch them change. Spending time with plants will make you realize how amazing life is.) People will pay for babysitting, housekeeping, errand running, or to have a personal trainer.

Fitness buffs, this is a great way to make money when you're young and just starting out. I know several people who pay a thousand dollars a month for their personal trainers. Get several of these clients, and you're financially free, flexible, and staying fit while doing it. This is crafting a life by your rules. It's not as though it's easy, however. It will take work and dedication to get clients and show your professionalism and commitment to their success. But that journey will be character-building and give you many learnings.

So, there are many ways you can earn money if you want to earn money to add to your micro-investing account. Maybe you get an allowance and want to forgo some of your fun spending and put 50 percent in your Acorns fund. Or maybe instead of spending the cash grandma and grandpa send you for your birthday and holidays, you invest it instead, or just invest a portion of it. Remember, even if you decide to put five dollars out of twenty into your micro- investing account, that's better than nothing. It's a start. And the start is what creates the snowball. Once you see that number rising, you will be inspired to add more. It's so nice when you start seeing your money make money. That's the biggest lesson that I was never taught: to let my money make money.

Let Your Money Make Money

Do you know what I would give now to have that wisdom at your age and the technology to do it? In my early and mid-twenties, I made way more money than I needed to keep my lovely one-bedroom apartment in Los Angeles afloat. There was never a conversation in my house growing up about investing. I just literally was so naïve that investing was never a thought in my mind. Having a lot of money certainly was. But I thought I had to make millions to be a millionaire. I didn't realize that money could make money, and I didn't have to do all the work. My young mind thought I would always have a lot of money. I thought large sums of money would always be offered to me, so I spent all my money. Saving wasn't a thought in my head either. It was a fun and fancy time. I have many great memories of my youthful splendor, BUT if I had invested that money, my life in my thirties and forties would have been supported in a much better way.

In the wonderful book *The Automatic Millionaire* by David Bach, he tells the story of how a couple who never made more than fifty thousand dollars a year retired as millionaires by keeping a diligent investment structure to their budget. This is super powerful information because it shows that even people who have very modest incomes can create wealth.

Bach tells the story of a woman who decided to forgo her daily Starbucks and put that in a fund instead and how a change like that can powerfully shift your financial trajectory. We tend to think small purchases don't matter, but time and money do amazing things—the five dollars turns into hundreds, even thousands in time.

These stories illustrate to us the significance of forgoing some unnecessary spending for your future wealth. It comes back to choice. We can choose to spend or invest. I am not saying never to spend. Spending offers many blessings as well. Create the balance. I had no balance. I spent everything extra that I made. I can say with certainty that I wasted a lot of money. That's a life lesson I guess I had to learn on my own. But you know better now.

Your choice to invest now means more choices for you in the future. We all want choices in life. Life sucks when there aren't choices. When you have more "have-tos" than "want-tos."

Imagine yourself in your twenties and thirties, armed with the financial security that your micro-investing endeavors have provided. You find yourself standing at a crossroads, faced with a momentous decision. On one path, there's the conventional route—a steady job with its own set of rules and limitations. On the other path lies the tantalizing opportunity to start your own business, a venture that could be the realization of your dreams.

Thanks to the financial foundation you've built through your investments, you have a real choice before you. It's not a decision driven solely by financial necessity but by your passions, ambitions, and desires. You have the freedom to listen to the beat of your own drum and to craft a life that aligns with your deepest values and aspirations. I read recently that 90 percent of adults aren't living congruently with their real desires. Your generation will change that. You won't stand for the ho-hum. Sure, you will likely have jobs in your teens and early twenties that will grow your character and experiences, but they may not be the most fun thing ever. But you won't have to live your life dissatisfied if you work smart.

Choosing to start a business can be both exhilarating and challenging. It's a path that requires determination, creativity, and resilience. But the beauty of having financial security from your investment fund is that it provides you with a safety net, reducing the fear and uncertainty that often accompany such leaps of faith. You have the means to invest in your ideas, to weather the inevitable storms that come with entrepreneurship, and to build something truly remarkable.

If you choose to embark on an entrepreneurial journey, you step into the realm of decision-maker, the captain of your own ship. You have the power to shape your destiny and create opportunities not just for yourself but for others as well. You become a creator, an innovator, and a leader in your chosen field.

But let's not limit the power of choice to starting a business alone. Financial security opens a plethora of possibilities. You may choose to travel the world, immersing yourself in new cultures and experiences. You might decide to further your education, pursue a passion, or engage in philanthropy to make a positive impact on the world.

Having the freedom to make these choices empowers you to live a life of fulfillment and purpose. You are no longer bound by the constraints imposed by financial insecurity. Instead, you're guided by your own aspirations and the desire to create a meaningful and fulfilling life for yourself.

It's important to remember that the power of choice doesn't just end with big decisions. Financial security grants you the freedom to make choices in your day-to-day life as well. You can prioritize experiences over material possessions, invest in your personal growth, and support causes that resonate with you. You can create a life that reflects your true values and priorities rather than being dictated by external pressures. The best part is you can pay people to do the things you don't want to do, helping others as well. Win-Win!

Micro-Investing Tools Mash-up

Let's start with the classic micro-investing tool, Acorns. With Acorns, you can connect your debit or credit card to automatically round up your purchases to the nearest dollar and invest the spare change. Say you spend five dollars and fifty cents on a slice of pizza—Acorns automatically transfers fifty cents into your investment fund. It's like having a squirrel tuck away your spare change for a rainy day! You literally start your investment funds with change you don't even know is gone when you invest it. Pretty awesome.

Acorns isn't the only option in this enchanted forest of micro-investing tools. There are others, each with their own magical powers and quirks:

1. ***Stash:*** Stash allows you to start investing with as little as five dollars and provides guidance and educational resources. It's like having a wise owl as your financial mentor. Just make sure to watch out for any hidden fees, as some features may have additional costs.

2. ***Robinhood:*** With Robinhood, you can invest in stocks, exchange-traded funds (ETFs), and even cryptocurrencies without any commission fees. It's like having your own fairy godmother granting you access to the world of investing. However, be cautious and do your research, as investing in individual stocks can be riskier than diversified portfolios.

3. ***Betterment:*** If you prefer a hands-off approach, Betterment might be the right choice for you. It uses

advanced algorithms to create a personalized portfolio based on your goals and risk tolerance. It's like having a magical forest sprite managing your investments. Just keep in mind that there may be annual fees associated with this service.

4. ***Wealthfront:*** Similar to Betterment, Wealthfront offers automated investing based on your preferences. It also provides additional features like tax-loss harvesting to optimize your returns. Think of it as having a team of diligent gardeners tending to your investment garden. However, note that Wealthfront has a minimum balance requirement to get started.

5. ***Stockpile:*** Stockpile is fantastic for creating investing knowledge for the entire family. Easily invests small amount. This is your handy investment assistant always there to make investing easy and fun for the whole family.

Remember, the key to micro-investing is consistency. By consciously choosing to invest a little here and there instead of mindlessly spending, you'll gradually build a bountiful garden of wealth. It's like watching a seedling grow into a magnificent tree, with each dollar you invest adding another ring of financial security.

Think of micro-investing as a game. Every time you resist the urge to splurge on something you don't truly need, you earn a point. And every dollar you save and invest is like leveling up in the game of wealth-building. So, go ahead, treat yourself occasionally, but remember to keep your eye on the grand prize: a financially secure future.

As you embark on this journey, you'll learn that it's not just about the money. It's about the satisfaction of taking control of your financial destiny, nurturing your investments, and watching them flourish. So, gather your spare change, my friends, and let's plant the seeds of wealth. You will grow a forest of financial success, one dollar at a time!

And always remember, even the mightiest oak tree started as a tiny acorn.

To break down some of the benefits of each micro-investing tool in an easy-to- digest way, here are some bullet points:

Acorns:

- *Automatically invests spare change from daily purchases.

- *Provides a simple and effortless way to start investing.

- *Offers diversified portfolio options based on risk preferences.

Stash:

- *Low minimum investment requirement, making it accessible for beginners.

- *Personalized portfolio options cater to various investment interests.

- *Educational resources help users learn about investing.

Robinhood:

- *Commission-free trading for stocks, ETFs, and cryptocurrencies.

- *User-friendly interface and easy account setup.

- *Provides opportunities for both long-term investing and active trading.

Betterment:

- *Automated investment management tailored to individual goals.

- *Offers tax-loss harvesting to optimize returns (you may want that if you start a business someday).

- *Provides goal-based planning and guidance.

Wealthfront:

- *Automated investment strategies designed for optimal returns.

- *Tax-efficient features to minimize tax liability.

- *No trading fees, making it cost-effective.

M1 Finance:

- *Enables customization of investment portfolios according to personal preferences.

- *Fractional shares allow for diversification with smaller amounts of money.

- *Combines automated investing with the ability to

choose individual stocks.

Ellevest:

- *Focuses on empowering women investors and addressing gender-specific financial needs.

- *Goal-based investing that considers factors like the gender pay gap and longer lifespans.

- *Provides personalized portfolios aligned with individual goals.

SoFi Invest:

- *Fractional shares allow investing with smaller amounts.

- *Provides commission-free trading and access to additional financial products.

- *Offers both active and automated investing options.

Stockpile"

- *Focuses on families saving and investing small amounts effortlessly.

- *Easy automatic transfers from linked accounts.

- *Ideal for beginners looking to start their investment journey.

Qapital:

- *Combines saving and investing with personalized rules.

- *Ideal for individuals seeking to achieve a set-and-forget approach to investing.

- *Encourages disciplined saving and investing habits.

Remember that while these micro-investing tools can be beneficial, it's crucial to carefully consider your investment goals, risk tolerance, and the fees associated with each platform. Each tool has its own unique features, and what works best for you depends on your individual financial situation and preferences. Always take the time to research and choose the option that aligns with your long-term financial goals.

So, Dear Teenager, as you cultivate your wealth through micro-investing, recognize the incredible power it gives you—the power to choose your own path, to chase your dreams, and to live life on your own terms. Embrace the possibilities and seize the opportunities that lie before you. Your future self will thank you for the choices you make today.

Now, go forth and plant tiny seeds! May you revel in the freedom that financial security provides, and may your journey be one of endless possibilities.

A Place To Write Notes

Chapter 6
Putting It All Together

Congratulations on learning how to cultivate your genius! Most people go their entire lives without learning what you have. You have read and embodied the Keys in this book, but it takes daily integration of these Keys to create magic. I recommend reading this book repeatedly until its teachings become seamlessly integrated into your ways of being. The morning routine, for instance, that is taught in Chapters 2 and 4, is something you must adopt and practice in order to receive the benefits it offers. Just like the gym analogy I used earlier, it only works if you go there and work out. Your morning routine only renders you amazing ongoing results if you "go there," meaning sit down and get still. And "work out," meaning focus your conscious attention on the feeling of your desired state.

It takes practice to wire your brain for confidence if you've experienced insecurity your whole life. It takes practice to feel abundant and supported if you've experienced lack most of your life. Give yourself the time and attention needed to wire into your subconscious mind whatever feelings you want to feel. Wire in the feeling of abundance, of love, friendship, security, creative fulfillment, all the things! Take time to consciously cultivate these feelings so they become very familiar. This is when amazing things show up in your life that match your vibrational offering of these elevated emotions.

Remember, too, that by doing this morning routine, you are creating optimal biochemistry in your system, keeping you at peak performance.

If you haven't already, pick up a copy of the *I Am Amazing Workbook for Teens.* This workbook is beautifully illustrated and full of writing prompts to get you acquainted with your own thread of genius. The questions take you on a journey to uncover your genius. The writing prompts are fun and give you a blueprint for what you really want in life and show you who you really are. Enjoy that beautiful and empowering journey.

Lastly, I meant it when I invited you to email me with your wins. I love to hear how the practices in this book transform people's lives. I learn from you when you let me be a witness to your manifestations, and it helps you to write down and share your wins. Your wins matter, and please don't discount things that you may consider small.

If you want to stay influenced by my content, sign up for my newsletter at www.BlytheNaturalLiving.com/teens. You can find me on Instagram at *@Blythemetz*, and on YouTube *@Blythe Natural Living*.

Recommend Reading List

Dear Teenager,

When I was nineteen years old, I read two books that would forever enhance my life. I know the power the right book offers the right reader. These books for me were *Anatomy of the Spirit* by Caroline Myss and *Women's Bodies, Women's Wisdom* by Christiane Northrup. I have not included these books in my list for you as they may be more tailored to my interests; however, by all means, read them if you feel called to them. The authors are legends in the world of women's health and empowerment.

I have put books on this list that I know will speak to your heart and empower you at this stage of your life. These books will help you stay connected to your power and support you in continuing to create a life you love. There are many more books that I recommend to adults in my programs; however, I don't want to risk you being bored by any book I recommend. For instance, I love the book *The Physics of Miracles: Tapping into the Field of Conscious Potential* by Richard Bartlett and all the books by Dr. Joe Dispenza, particularly *Becoming Supernatural.* However, these books are written for adults who have spent years, even decades, unconscious to their blocks. You, thankfully, have not spent decades unconscious to your blocks. I want to give you reading suggestions that speak to where you are now and will help support and serve you now in understanding your divinity and your inherent power. However, if you love neuroscience, those are amazing books to read.

The following books are tools for transformation, as I hope this book has been for you. They are all fun to read and will leave you stronger than you were before reading them. Enjoy, Dear One!

The Superconscious Path by Christopher Michael Duncan. This is a fiction story teaching non-fiction principles of how we create our lives through our conscious and unconscious choice and wounding. This is a fun and quick read, and the wisdom will stay with you and serve you.

A Happy Pocket Full of Money by David Cameron Gikandi. This book makes me smile every time I look at it, which is most days. After reading it cover to cover several times, I still love to plug into its wisdom and certainty every day, even for just a moment. It's a great book to pick up and read a page to set your mind right for the day. Powerful information that I wish I knew at your age.

The Code of the Extraordinary Mind by Vishen Lakhiani. This book is powerful. The author is the creator of Mindvalley, the largest personal transformation platform in existence. I highly recommend a yearly membership; there are quests from teaching you how to build a business to quests teaching you how to feng shui your space, to self-realization, to tantra, to fitness, and everything in between. This book is foundational information on unplugging from culturescape and tapping into your own genius seeking to express.

Awakened Imagination by Neville Goddard. Neville died before I was born, but his work continues to change my life. His teachings are so rich that sometimes I spend fifteen minutes just contemplating one sentence. Your life will be enriched in every way by putting into practice the information expressed in this and all his books. They may be a bit heady because they were written decades ago, and the English language has changed quite a bit; however, the brilliant message is clear.

Your Forces and How to Use Them by Christian D. Larson. This amazing book and several other life-changing books can be read for free at Psitek.net. This website is an amazing resource for reading books on self-improvement, spirituality, mind power, and personal growth, all for free and right at your fingertips. It's so great!

Metaphysics, New Dimensions of the Mind by Anthony Norvell. The first release of this book predates my birth, so like with Neville's books, the language seems old- worldly, which I love and think is fun to read. This is a scientific book that helps you understand how to use metaphysical principles to create amazing things in your life. Again, the principles in this book must be practiced with your focused mind in order to create the results suggested. This is a great book to read repeatedly to break free from programming that limits you.

A Return to Love by Marianne Williamson. I told a story in the previous pages about how I gave this book to a troubled boy many years ago. I read this book for the first time in my early twenties and think it's an excellent book for teens and young adults to read. It offers welcoming perspectives on life and relationships that open the heart and mind.

The Light We Carry by Michelle Obama. Our amazing former First Lady has created and continues to create initiatives that serve the youth. Her book, although not written for teens specifically, helps us all understand the light we carry and how to feel confident in sharing our light with others. Michelle Obama is an amazing person; her podcast is a great one to follow. Remember Chapter 4, staying influenced by those you admire. For me, Michelle Obama is someone I want to stay influenced by, and I think we all can learn a lot from her.

The Greatest Secret by Rhonda Byrne. You've likely heard of Rhonda's first massive-hit book and film movement entitled *The Secret,* in which the law of attraction is detailed. The latest installment in her collection can stand on its own as she pulls back the veil of perception that we all have been programmed to accept as reality. This book offers insights you can ponder for a lifetime and continue to receive new levels of awareness.

Explore TransformativePlays.org for a curated selection of plays crafted with your audience in mind. These stories resonate with the human spirit, offering narratives of triumph over adversity. Immerse your school, team, or organization in this collection of beautifully written plays, available as a unique fundraising product. Visit the website for more details and to download these empowering plays.

About The Author

Dr. Blythe Metz-Mändmets is a metaphysician, author, speaker, and holistic healing coach who specializes in helping her audience and clients REALize their self-healing design. She's passionate about helping youth and adults alike to understand their innate power to create the health and life experience they desire.

Join The Principles Program to learn how to create the health, vitality, and life YOU love.
www.BlytheNaturalLiving.com/ThePrinciplesSpecial

If you want to stay influenced by my content, sign up for my newsletter at www.BlytheNaturalLiving.com/teens.

You can find me on Instagram at @Blythemetz, and on YouTube @Blythe Natural Living.

Find other books by Dr. Blythe on Amazon: I Am Amazing Workboook For Teens, The SuperNatural Green Diet, Healthy Recipes In 5, and How to Work With Crystals

www.ingramcontent.com/pod-product-compliance
Lightning Source LLC
Chambersburg PA
CBHW052034150726
48002CB00002B/595